Landscaping with Native Texas Plants

Garden with gaillardia, coreopsis, shasta daisy (not native) in foreground, amorpha by water, yaupon holly and juniper in background, cedar elm overhead.

LANDSCAPING
with
Native Texas Plants

by Sally Wasowski *and* Julie Ryan

★

TexasMonthlyPress

Photographs used by the permission of the following: Carroll Abbott, Mr. and Mrs. Bob Burleson, Edith Bettinger, Robert L. Goodman, Geoffrey Stanford, Benny J. Simpson, Eric Tschanz, the San Antonio Botanical Center, the Fort Worth Botanical Center, the Dallas Museum of Natural History, the Heard Natural Science Museum and the Fort Worth Botanic Garden.

Texas Monthly Press, Inc.
P. O. Box 1569
Austin, Texas 78767

B C D E F G H

Library of Congress Cataloging in Publication Data

Wasowski, Sally, 1946—
 Landscaping with native Texas plants.

 Bibliography: p.
 Includes index.
 1. Landscape gardening—Texas. 2. Wild flower gardening—Texas. 3. Botany—Texas. 4. Plants, Ornamental—Texas. I. Ryan, Julie., 1948–
II. Title.
SB473.W37 1985 635.9'51'764 84-24034
ISBN 0-87719-004-6

Design by Whitehead & Whitehead

Printed in Japan by Dai Nippon Printing Co. Ltd. through DNP (America), Inc.

To my sweet, talented, handsome husband Andy,
who cooked meals, parented, washed dishes,
and rephrased everything I wrote,
including this dedication.—
Sally Wasowski

To Jimmie Jean Baldwin Ryan and Pat Ryan,
our parents and first guides to the glories of the outdoors,
and to my brothers and sisters:
Stuart, Suzanne, Claudia, James, and John.—
Julie Ryan

Contents

Preface

M Y CHILDHOOD HOME in the caprock country of northwestern Texas was landscaped quite simply, both in design and plant material used. All three trees and the single shrub were Asiatic in origin. The three Siberian elms were planted in a straight line in front of the house, and in one corner of the yard was a lone lilac bush. My grandmother was even more economical in her planting plan—there were only two Siberian elms in a straight line with, of course, the ubiquitous lilac. The sparsity of plant material was due primarily to three factors: a lack of availability of nursery-grown adapted trees and shrubs; a lack of time to care for trees and shrubs that did not produce a profit; and an absolute lack of water for supplemental irrigation. The shrub and trees might get some of the kitchen "gray water," if time permitted and it appeared they might die without water. There was no lawn, and if company was expected the yard was assiduously swept with a straw broom.

Yet, within a few miles of the yard fence, in almost any direction, was a wealth of adapted, attractive native plants. There were conifers—Rocky Mountain juniper, Pinchot juniper, and one-seed juniper. There were shade and flowering trees such as mesquite, western soapberry, and Mohr oak. Flowering shrubs and vines included fragrant mimosa, feather dalea, fragrant sumac, native grapes, and virgin's bower. There were even grasses for lawns—buffalo grass and curly mesquite grass. Many species of "wildflowers" grew in that 20-inch rainfall belt. Yet, little thought was given to transferring these waifs of the pastures and canyons to a formal landscape.

Why should we want to grow native plants? For many reasons! Many are extremely attractive and are adapted, within reason, to our environment. We have native plants of almost every shape, size, and form, although we are somewhat limited in broad-leaved evergreens and in plants that will grow in shade. Texas has many climates and soils, so not every native Texas plant can grow everywhere in the state. We have many plants from the western area of Texas that are extremely drought-tolerant, and we have a great number of plants from the east and west that can grow in waterlogged areas. I would caution against the idea that native plants in a landscape situation are going to be completely insect- and disease-free. They may or may not be free of pests, but this is something that only years of planting can tell us.

If natives are desirable and it makes such good sense to use them, why are they not used more in landscaping? Why are we in this situation of people being unable to purchase natives, on the one hand, and the nursery industry being unable to furnish native plants, on the other hand?

It is true that almost all the "class" trees available here *are* native—red oak, coast live oak, West Texas live oak, cedar elm, southern magnolia, sweetgum, flowering dogwood, Texas ebony, anaqua, wild olive, American holly, and yaupon holly, to name a few. But almost all our shrubs, turf, groundcover, and many of our vines are from foreign lands.

Up until the last five years, there was no great demand for native plants. Nursery people are simply not going to produce a plant that there is no market for. After all, they have employees to pay, taxes to render, children to school, and they would like to make a profit on their endeavors. Historically, we brought our plants with us from other areas and we wanted to bring a "piece of home" to this new land. Until a few decades ago, we were an agrarian society, and, in too many cases, most sadly, we were too busy with the clearing of this continent to appreciate its fragile ecology.

But times change—our cities are almost without water in the hot summer months and energy from fossil fuels has turned out to be finite. Not only do these fuels drive our mowers, but they also make our pesticides and nitrogen fertilizers. In consequence, many people are ready for a change in their lifestyles and in their home landscape.

Today we are an urban society, and nostalgia for the land as it once was with its climax flora is partially responsible for the popularity of the natives. It would seem, then, that the use of our own native plants for home beautification is an idea whose time has come. How refreshing that this book should come along at the same time! It is rather broad in its scope, for it touches on our prairie heritage of long ago and suggests how to use these plants in the actual landscaping of our city lots through the great prairie belt of Central Texas. These were the Blackland, Grand Prairie, and Cross Timbers. Texas is naturally a prairie state except for the Piney Woods of East Texas and the basins and ranges of the Trans-Pecos. I hope that the various plant lists and planting plans will be of value in the landscaping of your home or your business.

Benny J. Simpson
Texas Agriculture Experiment Station
Dallas, Texas 1984

Acknowledgments

M any people generously shared their technical advice, support, and professional services. We would particularly like to thank Benny J. Simpson at the Texas Agricultural Experiment Station at Dallas. Not only did he spend countless hours educating us, but he spent his summer vacation correcting the first draft of the book. The accuracy and quality of information here owes much to his expertise and vigilant eye. Edith Bettinger of the Native Plant Society of Texas, Dr. Geoffrey Stanford of Greenhills Environmental Center, Dallas, and Phil Huey, director of the Dallas Parks Department, put in nearly as many hours in going through the manuscript and sharing their experiences. Others who merit a very special mention here are David Riskind of Texas Parks and Wildlife, Austin; Ken Steigman of the Heard Natural Science Museum and Wildlife Sanctuary, McKinney; Mike Caspar of the Dallas Civic Garden Center; Marcia Coale of Wildflower Hotline, McKinney; Everett E. Janne of the Texas Agricultural Extension Service, Texas A&M University System, College Station; Marie Caillet of the Society for Louisiana Irises; Dr. David Diamond of the Texas Natural Heritage Program, Austin; Barney Lipscomb of the SMU Herbarium; the staff of the Dallas Museum of Natural History; and many others whose names you will find in the text.

We would like to thank Bob and Mickey Burleson, Temple, Texas, and Dr. Geoffrey Stanford, Greenhills Environmental Center, Dallas, for their written contributions to the prairie section.

For personal and technical assistance, Julie would like to thank Robert L. Goodman Photography, Dallas; members of Holy Cross Episcopal Church, Dallas; Judy Solganick, Dallas; and Dick Wood of Kingswood Computers, Dallas.

Though each photograph is credited individually, we would like to extend special thanks to the following institutions and individuals for so generously opening their slide collections to us: Benny J. Simpson; Dr. Geoffrey Stanford; Dr. Harold Laughlin; Heard Natural Science Museum and Wildlife Sanctuary; Edith Bettinger; Dallas Museum of Natural History.

Landscaping with Native Texas Plants

"What is a weed but a plant whose use has not yet been discovered?" (Emerson)

Introduction

IN THE 1980s the hardiness and resource conservation of the humble wildflower have gained much attention. Recent Texas winters and summer droughts have wreaked havoc on many familiar landscape plants. Ligustrums, Indian hawthorn, and pittosporum rattle in the breeze, brown and lifeless. A glance at your home water bill shows the cost of maintaining a typical lawn or garden—exorbitant, and getting higher every year. The strain affects more than the family pocketbook. As water demand grows, and the underground aquifers continue to dry up, we won't be able to spare 35 percent of the annual municipal water consumption for watering lawns and gardens (Texas Department of Agriculture estimate).

Only in recent years have a few original thinkers seen a solution right under our noses: native plants. Native plants aren't indestructible, but as a group they are hardier than exotics because they are adapted to their locales. After the record freeze of 1983–1984, the yucca bloomed in spring as it always has. Native yaupon kept its vivid red berries and glossy green leaves. In the Texas heat wave of 1980, roadside black-eyed susans and wild verbena kept their blooms; and in home gardens where they got a little water, they flowered profusely.

Native plants have gained popularity slowly but steadily since the early 1970s. Their proponents are a wide-ranging breed. They are landscape architects tired of the "knee-jerk" approach to landscaping that puts billiard-table–smooth lawns, crape myrtles, and a ligustrum hedge in front of home after home. They are conservationists who don't think it makes sense to maintain tropical grass lawns that may require up to 1.6 barrels of oil per acre each year in petroleum-based fertilizers. They are highway maintenance people who don't want to use $32 million of the state's annual highway budget to mow the roadside to the ground and administrators of cities like El Paso who can't afford to irrigate all of the city's public grounds. They are elderly people who remember the old-fashioned gardens of their childhood and wonder where the Turk's cap and clematis went—and young people who want a touch of the countryside in their city lot, and no mowing. They are disabled people who can't operate the power lawn mower and pruning shears necessary to tend our high-maintenance landscapes. And they are Texans—both newcomers and natives like Sally Wasowski and me—who feel a chill down our spines at the sight of a field ablaze with bluebonnets, a sensation that combines a thrill of home-pride with the tingle of spring's arrival.

Native plants, the ones that grow around us on the roadsides and vacant lots, and those that grow in old haymeadows and quiet woods where few of us see them, conserve resources because nature has spent thousands of years adapting them to Texas's varied soils and unpredictable climate. Planted in conditions similar to those of their original sites, they bring those conservation virtues with them. They offer local heritage, accumulating as they have the folk names our forebears gave them, and the lore of *curanderos* and pioneer doctors who unlocked their healing virtues. Some Americans are beginning to awaken from the old pioneer longing for New England and the Old World that gave us formal gardens of roses and tulips and to look with new eyes at Indian blanket, golden wave, and gayfeather.

Contrary to popular opinion, there is a greater variety of native garden plants adapted to Texas conditions than of introduced species. A mixture of the two can provide bloom nine months of the year and attractive foliage year-round. Native plants offer aesthetic appeal with their variety of shapes, colors, and textures. They lend themselves to looks ranging from casual to formal, lush to austere. Many successful native landscapes resemble natural settings, with a dash more color and style.

Lynn Lowrey, veteran horticulturist and native plant nurseryman for over thirty-five years, cites 1983 as the year he first felt the tide of interest in the commercial industry turn toward native plants. The Texas Department of Agriculture met with several major growers and native plant enthusiasts to see how the nursery industry and native plants in particular could get a boost. As a result of their meeting, a survey of the native trees stocked by 3,000 Texas growers is now available from TDA, soon to be followed by a more inclusive survey of several major plant categories. This is seen by Agriculture Commissioner Jim Hightower, nursery people, and enthusiasts as one step toward tapping a vast new agricultural market, not to mention conserving water and energy, and satisfying the rising demand for plants of the Southwest, inside the region and beyond. Native plants are one element in a $2 billion annual Texas nursery and florist market, 75 percent of which is supplied from out of state. Texas imports more wildflower seeds and plants than it exports, despite the fact that Texas has the third largest number of native species of any state. There are about 5,000 indigenous Texas species; 1,500 or more of them are the small blooming plants—popularly called "wildflowers"—that botanists call "forbs." Many species grow as far north as Kansas, and even into Canada. Others are akin to species in the same plant family that grow in one form or another throughout North America. Thus there is great potential for wider use of Texas plants.

A few hardy individuals who pioneered the field in relative anonymity since the 1950s are now leading the way for numerous institutions and groups to popularize native plants. Reliable propagation and culture information and consistent supplies of plants and seeds are important elements in the effort. The recently established National Wildflower Research Center east of Austin has as its first project a computer data bank to access a vast array of information on American wildflowers. The U.S.D.A. Soil Conservation Service tests and approves for release to the nursery industry both native and introduced shrubs, trees, and grasses at its three Texas research stations; currently about 60 percent of the plants under study are natives. The Texas Agricultural Experiment Station conducts a program headed by Benny J. Simpson that tests and approves conservation-wise native "woodies" or shrubs for the nursery industry. The Texas Department of Highways and Public Transportation has cut its annual $32 million mowing budget and at the same time bathed the roadsides in beauty, by reducing its highway right-of-way mowing and letting the wildflowers bloom and go to seed.

Many Texans' first memories of wildflowers date back to the time when they discovered ice cream, toad frogs, and tying their own shoes. By the time I was ten years old, my family had lived in Austin, Texas, and Levittown, New York, followed by the Texas towns of San Antonio, Victoria, and Dallas. From the byways of the Gulf Coast, I remember wild rose vines and winecups. In Victoria, we children nestled in the wild clover that grew behind our new home and listened to the bees buzz. On vacation travels, we plucked day primroses and rubbed their yellow pollen on each other's noses, calling them "buttercups" as many Texans do. Both our grandmothers had gardens. I recall the red-and-orange needle-point of lantana blooms and the "bleeding hearts" that grew in shady spots—as well as fruit trees and roses tended carefully against the West Texas sun and sand. Many people have memories of the plants and flowers of their childhood homes. In cherishing what was first dear to us, we keep that sense of home alive. For people to whom Texas is a new home, familiarity with native plants can give a sense of belonging. Newcomers, too, can learn to mark the seasons by the advent of redbud, bluebonnet, and gayfeather. Wildflower fans swarm like bees in spring at the state's wildflower festivals: Texas Wildflower Day at Texas Woman's University in Denton; Wildflower Trails of Texas at Linden, Avinger, and Hughes Springs; the Greenhills Wildflower Workshop in Duncanville in May; Austin's Flora-Rama; and Wildflower Day on Tridens Prairie west of Paris, to name only a few.

In this book we would like to introduce you to key people and groups who are working to make native plants available and understandable to more people. They form the network from which the field will grow. We present native examples from six plant categories: perennial flowers, shrubs, decorative trees, shade trees, vines, and grasses. Sally has selected native Texas plants that will grow in the limestone and blackland areas of the state and neighboring states. Her garden plans illustrate their uses. In addition, we will introduce you to the Blackland Prairie region that extends from Grayson, Fannin, Lamar, and Red River counties in Northeast Texas down to the San Antonio area, and covers two oblong "islands" between the Waco–San Antonio axis and Houston. The Blackland Prairie was the original source of many wildflowers used in gardens, as well as native grasses that are only beginning to get the attention they deserve as landscape plants.

We hope that this book will bring to the public a dialogue that has gone on within earshot of only a few. By word-of-mouth, newsletters, and scientific journals, plantsmen and plantswomen have shared their information for years. We have been listening in, and we want to share what we've heard with you. We thank them for their generous sharing of research and slide collections, and for their blessing that we now extend to you: "Grow good!"

Eric Tschanz

Cabins like this dotted the Texas countryside in pioneer days. This early home was reassembled in the native area of the San Antonio Botanical Center and surrounded with pine, magnolia, oak, and sweetgum.

2

Native Plant Pioneers

IN A WORLD in which the same tall, scarlet spike of bloom may be called "standing cypress," "Texas plume," or "red-hot poker," and those same names are applied to other unrelated flowers, one eventually submits to the necessity of learning at least a few plants' scientific names—or else to complete confusion. A discovery follows: native Texas plants have two botanical names, like other plants, and the second one is often something strange like *lindheimerii* or *drummondii*, as in *Opuntia lindheimerii* or *Phlox drummondii*. That is simply because the plants in question are the species of *Opuntia* cactus that was discovered by Lindheimer and "Drummond's phlox."

As early as the 1820s, pioneer naturalists were busy exploring Texas and identifying new plants. Dr. Edwin James accompanied the Long Expedition to the Texas Panhandle in 1820 and collected plant specimens. The Teran Expedition along the Texas-Mexico border between 1826 and 1834 included a French botanist, Berlandier. Thomas Drummond was a Scottish botanist who collected 700 species of plants in Southeast Texas. The list goes on. New plants continue to be discovered, such as the *Salvia greggii* variety "Abbott's white," identified by Mark Abbott of Kerrville in 1981. But pioneers in the field of native plants now look primarily for answers to questions about culture, propagation, and uses in landscapes and agriculture. The question "What is it?" is pretty well answered, compared to "How do I grow it; where do I get it; do I start it from seeds, cuttings, or transplants—and what good is it, anyway?" And none of these answers is much good until it gets to the people who want to know: growers; nursery people; landscape architects, designers, and contractors; public agencies; farmers and ranchers; and home gardeners—so publication of information on native plants and publicity on their merits are also pioneering efforts. We would like to introduce you to some of the people who have carried on where Drummond and Lindheimer left off. First let's look at the heritage into which they were born—the green heritage of Texas flora and plant culture, and Texans' attitudes toward it.

To early settlers, "garden" brought to mind plants as diverse as the cultures they had left behind: old-fashioned gardens of assorted perennials; the Deep South's azaleas and "Cape jasmine"; and, to the affluent few, formal gardens in the English style. To many, "garden" meant vegetables. Ornamentals were an unnecessary luxury. Certainly many settlers must have tucked a favorite hardy shrub, or some root stock, or a handful of seeds into their wagon loads. From exploring the remnants of abandoned gardens around old homes, it seems that native Texas flowers and shrubs of prairie and woods, as well as introduced species, were used in early gardens in the state. Much later, when the standard of living had risen above subsistence level and the nursery industry had begun to develop, more choices were available. Since the 1950s, popular taste and the nursery and chemical industries have conspired to foster American gardens that are showy, labor-intensive, and dependent on lavish supplies of water, pesticides, herbicides, and petroleum-based fertilizers. Some native plants, such as composite flowers like the daisies, were scientifically bred for gardening and "improved." Native trees were the most widely used indigenous plant group, as they are still. For the most part, native flowers other than the "improved" varieties were ignored. Hybrid and exotic ornamental plants were considered the only garden plants worthy of the name.

Many people in the hard-scrabble early Texas days had neither energy nor money to spare for flowers, shrubs, and trees, unless they sprang up on their own and grew untended. Field flowers were undesirable, to many minds. "They were fighting life," Benny Simpson says of his family on the Rolling Plains of Texas. "They battled those weeds in the field—it never would have occurred to them to put them in the yard." Many people in the arid regions of Texas simply raked their bare yards. Lack of water was another factor. Nothing grew on the cleared land without hauling water to arouse the land's sleeping fertility. The early Texans were here to subdue the wilderness, not to join forces with it.

Now a more open attitude toward native plants prevails. The science of ecology, which developed out of study of the native American prairie from 1895 to the 1940s, percolated into popular awareness over the years, enabling people to see natural areas as finely balanced, interdependent communities, not as mere assortments of plants and animals, the viewpoint that had prevailed in prior centuries. "Ecology" and "ecosystem" entered the vocabulary. The new science and the obvious effects of pollution and intensive development on our natural surroundings sparked greater concern for native species and communities. Increasing urbanization, and standardization in all aspects of life, whetted the public taste for the antique and the rustic in home architecture and interiors, styles complemented by native plants. Conservation of petroleum, on which contemporary landscape management depends heavily, became a national priority after crises like the OPEC oil blockade of 1974. The American Bicentennial prompted a new look at our national heritage in all areas, including the land itself. Thus many projects involving native plants and wilderness areas, such as wildflower trails, were launched in honor of the Bicentennial. All in all, the material and psychological demands of the times aroused greater interest in the natural world. The moment came for indigenous plants to be considered on their own merits, and for the work of evaluating them for a wide range of uses to expand and gain recognition.

The few lone Texas plantsmen and plantswomen who researched native grasses, flowers, shrubs, vines, and trees labored mostly unknown in the 1940s, 1950s, and 1960s. They worked in home gardens and test plots. Some conducted research over many years. A few approved tested plants for release to the nursery industry. Those who were to become the Texas native plant movement were then a widely scattered, dimly visible constellation. Word of their work passed mostly by word-of-mouth among interested individuals. Then, in the 1970s, the time was right for "wild" plants to come in from the wilderness, and for the native plant people to come in from the cold. Their numbers increased; seminars and newsletters multiplied; interest grew.

Native plant enthusiasts in Texas are as diverse as the flora. In fact, they are fairly similar to it in several respects. They're individualists, they're well adapted to the areas in which they live, and they beautify their locales. Many grew to be what they are now without benefit of a university education. They embarked on their careers without assurance that anyone would pay them for it—many are "volunteers." They subsist on scant resources. When you leave their company, you are likely to take something with you that will take root and sprout.

Contacts with informed plantspeople are possible through many organizations and institutions: the Native Plant Society of Texas, garden clubs, natural history museums, nature preserves, experiment stations, nurseries. We would like, in a brief space, to introduce you to only a few of the individuals and organizations involved in bringing native plants into landscape use. The seven people you will meet have a broad range of backgrounds: home gardening, science, horticulture, public relations. They illustrate the diversity of the field. Their contributions are stated all too briefly here. In the broad state of Texas, as they themselves point out, there are others with dedication, experience, and scientific training equal to and possibly surpassing their own. I only wish that in my brief involvement to date in the native plant world I had met all the knowledgeable "plant pioneers," and could introduce you to them all. Let these few be our first guides.

Lynn Lowrey, Louisiana-born plantsman, specialized in native plants for thirty-five years at his own nurseries in Houston, Conroe, and New Braunfels, and later in Brenham. He is the one native plant aficionado everyone says a person must see to know what native plants are really about. And see one must, because Lowrey is a shy man of very few words. Joe Bradberry of Lone Star Growers, a new commercial nursery in San Antonio, recognized Lowrey's authority in the field after a few meetings and invited him to head Lone Star's research and development program. After six months in the job, Lowrey had 400 species of native plants under cultivation, including 30 vivid species of salvia, other wildflowers, flowering trees, grasses, and shrubs. He and Bradberry anticipate having 10,000 containerized plants ready for the wholesale market in 1985 and 100,000 within three years. Lone Star joins other Texas growers like Aldridge of San Antonio in seeking to meet the demands of a broadening native plant market.

Benny Simpson, research scientist at Texas Agricultural Experiment Station at Dallas, has worked for over thirty-five years with native plants. Since 1972, he has concentrated on selecting resource-efficient species for release by A&M to the nursery industry. A recent Simpson release is "Thunder Cloud" cenizo, a lovely, gray-foliaged dwarf shrub that bears clouds of purple blooms after rainy spells.

Dr. Barton Warnock, professor emeritus of Sul Ross College in Alpine, writes full-color guides to the flora of the Trans-Pecos region of Texas. His books are based on fifty years of collecting trips through this semidesert and desert area that contains more species of native plants than any other part of Texas. "He is one man I know who's welcome on any ranch in that part of the country," says fellow plantsman Lynn Lowrey. Dr. Warnock devotes his

Julie Ryan

Experimental gardeners Kay Warmerdam and Edith Bettinger in Kay's suburban garden-with-a-difference.

time to surveying the native plants of the region and continues to identify new ones. At present he is developing a four-acre native shrub garden on a private ranch near Marathon. He will also identify the plants installed at the Lajitas Museum and Desert Garden, expected to be a showcase of Trans-Pecos flora.

Garden clubs in Texas have played a role in promoting wildflowers. "Don't think we're just the ladies who plant petunias in the wrong places and drink tea," admonishes Mary Kittel, a fifty-year veteran of garden clubs who served as president of the National Council of State Garden Clubs from 1973 to 1975. Comprised of approximately half a million members from every state in the union and an equal number of international affiliates throughout the world, the garden clubs' national council promotes the use of indigenous plants in both private and public landscapes.

Although Mary Kittel no longer has a garden, she experiments with a piñon pine on the windswept balcony of her high-rise condominium overlooking Fort Worth's Botanic Garden and continues to promote garden club programs, including natural habitat preservation and education.

As for people actively involved in getting field flowers into the home landscape, one could hardly find more avid experimental gardeners than Kay Warmerdam of Lewisville and Edith Bettinger of Flower Mound. "In the past ten years, Edith and I have probably worked with over 100 species of flowers, grasses, and shrubs," estimates Mrs. Warmerdam. As Wildflower Preservation chair for the Garden Clubs of Texas, Inc., and founding president of the Native Plant Society of Texas, she is in a position to spread their findings around. Her garden originated when, after her husband's death, she moved off the farm they had owned and took with her most of the plants in the farmhouse front yard. Her back garden is a traditional St. Augustine–carpeted lawn, ringed by a

Julie Ryan

Joe Bradberry and horticulturist Lynn Lowrey (rear, left to right) work to bring native plants into the nursery industry at Lone Star Growers, with staff members (clockwise) Chris Colasono, Agnes Hubbard, and David Sabalka, seen here in the nursery's native plant research section.

garden border and centered with an oval raised bed of live oaks, ornamental trees, and an array of native and introduced flowers and shrubs. There are three showy blue- and magenta-flowered spiderwort species, horsetail reeds, salvias in shades from white to red and blue, a rare *Spiranthes* orchid, and scores of other plants. Small name plates are tucked into the soil here and there. Elsewhere in the garden are native prairie grasses used as border plants, a mustang grape vine on the fence corner, giant cone-flowers 8 feet tall, and "lamb's ear" mullein 5 feet high and flower-ing with blooms almost as showy as those of yucca, but yellow. Between the two of them, Warmerdam and Bettinger informally supply scores of people with information, seeds, and cuttings. Experimentation is vital, they agree. "You never know if a wild plant will fail or take over your garden when you give it better soil and more water," says Mrs. Bettinger, who is an active partici-pant in the Native Plant Society and in the historic prairie pre-served by the town of Flower Mound. Mrs. Bettinger maintains a naturalistic woodland setting on her treed lot. She and Kay Warmerdam are two of the many home gardeners developing the culture information necessary for successful use of native Texas plants by homeowners and landscape professionals.

In the Hill Country, Carroll Abbott turned his public relations and publishing skills, along with hard-won horticultural know-how, to the cause of native plants for thirteen years. His public relations efforts had helped launch several notable Texans, includ-ing Governor John Connally, Ray Roberts in his four congres-sional campaigns, and Ben Barnes, later lieutenant governor. Wildflowers figured in his earliest childhood memories. During the 1960s, they brightened the weary campaign trail. When he no-ticed they were dwindling as development encroached, and the Texas Legislature's response to his continued pleas for protection, promotion, and research funding was lukewarm, he went home to Kerrville at the age of forty-four and entered a new line of work: landscaping with native plants. He talked clients into using natives. Then he dug the plants from bar ditches and the land of obliging farmers, a time-consuming, hit-or-miss process—but there was no other source. He harvested seed from the highways and byways. Before long, he was running a mail-order seed house called Green Horizons out of the family's concrete house on the Guadalupe River, reportedly the first native seed company in Texas.

In time, Green Horizons also produced a newsletter of culture information on the plants. Then Abbott printed his now popu-

Doug Milner

Carroll Abbott, with his "Beautiful, Beautiful Texas" wildflower calendar.

lar "Beautiful, Beautiful Texas" wildflower calendar. After several years he wrote and published *How to Know and Grow Texas Wildflowers*. The cold turndowns he received marketing it to bookstores threw him back on the expertise of his newspapering years and led to the mail-order approach Green Horizons now relies on.

Now the Green Horizons mailing list has grown to 30,000 names. Texas Wildflower Day is on the calendar, the first Saturday after San Jacinto Day, as a result of lobbying by Abbott and Dr. Mary Evelyn Huey, president of Texas Woman's University. Green Horizons' catalog now lists scores of book titles, free seed offers, culture information, wildflower notepaper, and floral Texana of all kinds.

Abbott's death in 1984 at the age of fifty-seven left a legacy for Texas. The newsletter continues under the editorship of his wife Pat and son Mark. Green Horizons was, you might say, the seed-bed of the statewide native plant movement. And if you want to think of the native plant movement not as a garden but as, say, a circus, Carroll Abbott was its P. T. Barnum, the man who beat the drum to draw the public and gave the gorgeous wildflowers the spotlight they deserve.

This garden, photographed in August, was planted the previous April. The native plants in bloom are ironweed, black-eyed susan, hardy verbena, and prairie verbena.

Growing Native Plants

INTRODUCTION

THERE'S AN OFTEN quoted line from Saint John—something about a prophet having no honor in his own country. Every time I hear that reference, I can't help but think about the native plants of Texas.

I suppose it's just human nature. We tend to take the familiar and commonplace for granted. In landscaping, the old rule seems to have been, if it's "exotic" and imported, then it's more desirable than any of our home-grown native plants. You might be surprised to hear that many of our native plants are being cultivated in Europe as exotics. In Japan, our plants are very popular; that's appropriate, since most of our nursery stock is Japanese.

Happily, there is a new and growing trend in landscaping—a burgeoning recognition and appreciation for our own native flora. We find indigenous plants being used more frequently in home gardens and, yes, even on commercial properties—with good reason. Our natives have a staying power that most of the imports can't begin to match. If you drove around Dallas the spring following the big freeze of 1983–1984, as I did, then I can rest my case. You saw the heavy toll in non-native trees and shrubs, flowers, and groundcovers. The casualty list was long and included such favorites as wax leaf ligustrum, Indian hawthorn, and dwarf nandina. They just can't handle our weather extremes.

Here in North Central Texas, we experience a range of temperatures that can give us long spells of 115° F days to winter chills that drop down to 5° F. We have long periods of little or no rain that would challenge the survival instincts of a camel. It takes a very special, very hardy plant not only to survive here, but to thrive in these extreme conditions. But if all they had to recommend them was an ability to "take it," then our native plants would not be seeing this upsurge of interest. Many offer some of the most eye-appealing flowers and foliage you could desire.

If you landscape with natives, your garden can boast vibrant and colorful explosions of *Zexmenia* and *Ungnadia*, or delicate displays of *Pavonia* and *Anisacanthus*. Our natives offer a wide spectrum of exciting colors and textures and fragrances. Rest assured, your creative instincts will have a full and varied palette to utilize when you plan your garden.

Each plant in this book was selected because it possessed some characteristic not available in our current nursery stock. Almost without exception, these plants grow in limestone, caliche, and black prairie muck. And, for the most part, they will also grow in sandy soil. Most are drought-tolerant. Several bloom all summer, not minding our hot spells, provided you give them *some* water. All but a few are winter-hardy down to 5° F, and those exceptions are noted in the plant descriptions.

The list of decorative trees is perhaps the most important part of this book. Despite the big demand for trees of this size, nurseries typically carry less than ten varieties, half of them not suited to our climate. What a shame, when there are so many other exciting possibilities!

The concept of the perennial garden, well established in Europe and South America, has never really caught on here. The reason is simple—most of the perennials used in those gardens will not take our Texas heat, or will bloom only in May and not all summer. I specialize in designing all-year, low-upkeep perennial gardens using Texas native plants—the only way to pull it off here. I recently revisited one of these gardens. It had not rained in a month, and the temperature was in the nineties. There were cracks in the ground half an inch wide. Still, three-fourths of the garden was in full bloom, and the later-blooming plants were green and healthy.

To give you a better idea of how to use native plants, I've drawn up a few sample gardens; if you were to hire a landscape designer, you would receive a plan similar to these layouts, tailored to your specific home and yard. One of the plans is for a Texas-style rock garden, using plants that are especially heat- and drought-resistant. There is also a bird garden for those who want to attract birds to their home. Another is a shady perennial garden. It's for older homes with shady yards that still want color in the summer. Then there is a plan on how to make your own woods, complete with understory—all the small trees and shrubs and vines that grow under the big shade trees. If you make your own woods, you can choose blooming plants for your under-story, making a very beautiful wooded plot in spring and fall. My fifth plan is in the style of a Mexican patio garden, with a fountain, potted plants, and a pergola, for the condominium-sized yard.

With the plans I have also included lists that I find useful when-ever I am designing a garden. These group the plants in accordance with bloom times, watering needs, and shade. Though I have used only native plants in these schemes, in order to show a use for nearly every plant in this book, in real life I usually like to mix natives with other plants that are readily available in area nurseries and seem to do exceptionally well in our area, in spite of being "foreigners."

The last two chapters are about a very different kind of land-scaping—prairie. My co-author, Julie Ryan, has prepared a section of ideas and information on how to use our native grasses as ornamental plants or in a prairie garden. If you think really big, there are some tips on how to begin turning worn-out grassland into reconstructed prairie. After the prairie garden plan, there is a section on how to grow a buffalo grass lawn. If you don't like to water, you don't want to mow, and you have full sun, this might be the lawn for you.

I am well aware that this book is in no way the last word on native plants for landscaping. For one thing, these plants are not standardized like the nursery plants we are used to. Until they do enter the nursery trade, you will never know for sure how tall they will grow or how big the flowers will be or, in some instances, even what color! Different gardeners can have spectacular successes or failures with the same plant. They might also find, upon closely comparing the plants in question, that although they are correctly identified as being the same plant, they may differ greatly in size, color, and beauty.

As you go through this book, you may discover that I've in-cluded a plant you happen to loathe, or excluded one you love. First of all, I found that space did not allow me to use all of *my* favorites. Second, some plants that have sentimental value for many people have particular landscaping problems. For example, the sycamore (*Platanus occidentalis*), beautiful in the river bottoms with its white bark, gets scorched leaves and loses limbs in the summer when planted on dry land, even in a well-watered yard.

One last but very important note: my landscaping business took off in the direction of native plants as a result of a course on the subject that I took at Texas Woman's University, taught by William Beale. He'd arranged to have several guest lecturers, the most memorable being Benny Simpson from the Texas Agricultural Experiment Station in Dallas and the late Carroll Abbott of Green Horizons. Both of these men were already legendary in the field, universally considered "gurus" of native plant lore. It is certain that, if it had not been for these men and the enthusiasm they engendered in me, I would never have found myself writing this book.

THE QUEST FOR NATIVE PLANTS

After you've finished reading this book, you'll no doubt want to include a number of these plants in your landscaping plans. Call your local nursery first. If they don't carry what you want, tell them that they should. Then contact the Texas Department of Agriculture for their directory of nurseries that do carry native plants. See Sources for the address and for other ideas of where to look, such as the Texas Native Plant Society. This is a wonderful place to exchange plants and seeds, as well as information. There is a local chapter for each part of the state.

Still another source for native plants is growing your own. The two main ways are by seed and by cuttings. I do not recommend that you dig up plants by the highway. That is against the law. Those plants are maintained for all the public, not just you. Even on private land where you have the necessary permission from the owner, it is better to gather seed than to dig. You really don't want to destroy the very flowers you appreciate—and destroy you will, because very few ever survive being transplanted bare root, especially while conspicuous with flowers or seed.

You can buy seed from one of the many sources listed in the back of this book or from any other source you may find on your own. You should know that the further away from you the seed was gathered, the more it is going to differ from your native population. If you have the time and inclination, you can learn to gather your own seed. "Shop around" in nearby fields, developers' lots, and, believe it or not, cemeteries and near railroad tracks. Wild plants have active gene pools and can vary considerably; some have larger flowers or prettier colors or finer leaves than the same plant in the next field. Find the prettiest one while it is in bloom or showing fall colors. Then mark it, so you can find it when you return for the seeds. Remember, also, that a small plant—lonely on a limestone outcrop—might grow twice as big in your garden, its size being a result of environment rather than genetics.

If you plan to go this route, I advise you to buy Carroll Abbott's book *How to Know and Grow Texas Wildflowers*. There are two recent professional books on propagation techniques. One is by Dr. Ed McWilliams of Texas A&M, a research scientist. The other is by Jill Nokes, who has combined scientific research with hands-on experience as a propagationist with Native Sun Nursery in Austin.

NOTES ON PLANT INFORMATION

Latin Names

Plants have been listed with double Latin names ever since the Swedish botanist Carolus Linnaeus started the system back in 1753. The first name signifies the genus, the second name signifies the species. Although these names may change on occasion, it is still the most precise method of universal identification. For example, if your landscape plan calls for *Salvia greggii* and you buy *Salvia farinacea*, you'll wind up with a blue-flowered herb instead of the red-flowered shrub originally intended.

Pronunciation

Now that you know the Latin names are important, don't panic. I really don't think it's vital that you use impeccable pronunciation when discussing these plants at your local nursery. But it *is* important to get used to their strange-sounding "official" names for ordering, planning, and research. If you don't try to pronounce them, you won't remember them. If you already pronounce the names another way, don't worry about it. The fact is, after we slap our English long vowel sounds on them, Julius Caesar himself wouldn't recognize his native tongue. There seem to be a lot of variations in pronunciation. In producing my guide, I've consulted several books and dictionaries and Mike Kaspar of the Dallas Garden Center.

Common Names

Most plants have a common name—often more than one. I have listed only the one or two most often used. Sometimes a common name can refer to more than one species of plant, which really confuses matters. That's when those good old Latin names can straighten things out. The rain lily is an example. *Habranthus texanus*, *Zephyranthes pulchella*, and *Cooperia drummondii* are all called "rain lily." Each has very distinct characteristics.

Height

This refers to the ultimate height a plant will attain. With trees, it can take twenty years to a century to reach maximum growth. Most perennials take two years. Some of these heights might vary with soil and water conditions and length of growing season.

Spacing

Essentially, this refers to the width of the plant. When you read planting instructions and see the reference "3 feet on center" this does not mean the plants should be placed 3 feet apart, although in mass plantings it turns out that way. Reserve an area 3 feet by 3 feet square, and place each plant directly in the center of that spot, which gives it adequate room to develop while still blending in with adjacent plantings. Always measure the distances between plants from the center of one plant to the center of the nearest plant.

Bloom Time

The period when the plant is most likely to put forth flowers. This time can vary. For instance, in a hot dry spring, buds might appear during the first half of the bloom time; in a cold spring, during the second half. In a mild, damp spring, the plant might bloom during the entire period. Cutting off old blooms (thereby preventing the plant from going to seed) and watering can usually extend the blooming time. Also, if your plant is in a sunny, protected spot, it might bloom two weeks prior to your neighbor's identical plant located in a cool, shady place. This is true of all plants, by the way, not just natives.

Range

This information is listed to give people a good idea as to whether or not a particular plant will grow well in their gardens. Actually, slightly out of habitat is often best; the growth of the plant is sometimes a little restrained if you are going from moister to drier conditions, which makes a plant like lantana more manageable. Also, insects that feed on a particular plant might not be present in the new location. *Myrica cerifera* can be defoliated by leaf-cutter ants in East Texas, but we don't have that problem in Dallas.

Perennial

A plant that returns to the same spot year after year because the roots do not die when the leaves drop. Some perennials are evergreen.

Biennial

A plant that takes over twelve months to bloom and then dies after setting seed. Some will "bolt," which means that they will bloom early.

Annual

A plant that dies at the end of the year and must be replaced, either by planting a new one or by growing it from seed.

Sun

The plant needs or will do well in sun all day long.

Part Sun

A minimum (or maximum) of four to six hours of sunshine each day. Some plants can span Sun to Part Sun, or Part Sun to Dappled Shade. If the latter, the four–six hours of sun should be the maximum.

Dappled Shade

Filtered sun light or bright patches or splashes of light coming through a tree or trellis most of the day.

Shade

Less than four hours of sun a day.

Propagation

Methods of reproduction which are generally successful.

Germination

The number of days it usually takes for the first two leaves to show after planting the seed at optimum soil temperature. If you are starting the seed inside with bottom heat, you can heat the medium to the proper temperature. Otherwise, if you are planting directly in the ground, the germination time might be delayed if the soil is too cool.

Categories

The plants are listed according to use rather than by their taxonomy. For example, some shrubs are listed for use in a perennial garden because they flower well and are fairly small. Others are listed under shrubs, because they are used more for their foliage and are larger. However, some (such as *Anisacanthus wrightii*) could go equally well in either category, so their placement was purely arbitrary; I moved them back and forth until it was too late to change the copy. Some other shrubs are listed as decorative trees, because they are large and ungainly as shrubs and beautiful as trees. But, again, this is an arbitrary categorization; many of these, if left unpruned, make a lovely boundary hedge for an estate-sized lot. *Rhus virens* does equally well as a hedge or a small tree. I vacillated quite a while on its placement before it settled in shrubs. The naturalizing plants are another gray area. Many plants that sucker (send out roots to produce new plants) are not in that section because, in my judgment, they do not spread as badly or they have a redeeming quality—but that is subjective. These categories reflect my experiences, and if they do not reflect yours, please carry on with what works for you.

Soils

BLACKLAND PRAIRIE. This type of soil is deep and calcareous, meaning that there is an excess of available calcium, usually in the form of the compound calcium carbonate or "lime." Sometimes these soils have caliche—a crust of calcium carbonate that forms when there is not enough rain to wash the calcium away. Caliche is found most often in dry rocky places where the soil is not deep. Black prairie soil is very rich and does not need fertilizing, unless you want to add cottonseed meal or something else high in phosphate to promote more bloom. The clay content makes it sticky when wet and hard as concrete when dry. The higher the clay content, the more the soil will shrink when dry, making big cracks in the ground and leaving the foundation of your house standing without support. The soil also shrinks around the roots of the plants, helping their roots to stay moist.

To make this soil easier to work, water deeply for two to three hours. Then let it dry out for two to three days. It should then be crumbly and friable. If you want to loosen the soil more permanently, I've found that digging in bark mulch and sharp sand keeps the soil easily workable for a number of years. Peat moss seems to disappear in one year.

LIMESTONE. Texas used to be covered with warm shallow seas which deposited lime-bearing muds to form limestone. This happened many times and composed many layers. The Cambrian and Ordovician layers, 600 million to 400 million years old, now hold our principal reserves of oil and gas in West Texas. In the Permian, a little over 250 million years ago, West Texas was a large inland sea with limestone reefs more than a mile thick. These now form the Guadalupe Mountains. Most of the exposed limestone in

Texas is from the Cretaceous, 140 million to 70 million years ago. These limestones contain many fossils. Those laid down in the Lower Cretaceous, like the Austin chalk, are harder and erode more slowly. Much of the softer Upper Cretaceous has already worn away to form our limy soils.

Plants that can grow out of limestone have root systems that penetrate tiny crevices in the rock to seek out the water stored there. Exposed limestone is usually at the tops of hills and near gravel pits and stream beds, where the top soil has been washed away until it is very thin or nonexistent.

To plant a tree in limestone, loosen as much rock as you can and add mulch to fill in around the root ball. Water frequently and deeply, because the soil does not retain water; until the roots have had time to grow into the rock, the tree is dependent on your watering to stay alive.

ACID SANDS. East Texas has sandy, acid-reacting soil. This is typical of the land all across the South. Plants that grow in this environment generally get chlorosis in limy soils, an iron deficiency evident when the leaves start turning yellow in hot weather. These plants usually require more water, having gotten used to the higher rainfall levels in this part of the state. The only exception to this rule is in the drier parts of the Cross Timbers and some parts of South Texas. The other sandy areas in the state are usually neutral or basic in reaction. Since people who live in East Texas already get to have dogwood, azaleas, camellias, and gardenias with no trouble, I have not included plants exclusive to their area in this book. Many of their plants do grow in the rest of the state and can be found in this book.

Water

RAINFALL. Rainfall varies considerably in Texas, from over 50 inches a year in East Texas to less than 12 inches a year in the Trans-Pecos. The Blackland Prairies average 30–40 inches and the Cross Timbers 25–32 inches. The Edwards Plateau averages 15–33 inches a year. Texas gets progressively drier the further west you go. That makes sense. Everybody knows that Louisiana is wetter than New Mexico. Rain is usually heaviest in May and September for most areas, but in Texas you can never depend on rain.

WATERING. When you start a plant from *seed*, the ratio between roots and leaves will always be correct. When you buy a *container plant* from the nursery, it will need careful deep watering for a whole year to get fully established. It is better to let the hose run on a plant for fifteen minutes than to sprinkle it for thirty minutes. Sprinkling wets only the top few inches at the most. If it has been a long time since there was a good soaking rain, it is possible to have a dry stratum of soil between the damp surface and the moist soil where the roots should be. This encourages a young plant to keep its roots at the surface, making it entirely dependent on your sprinkling. A one- to two-hour watering is best, to get water down deep into the soil where you want the roots to grow. If it is very dry, water an hour one night and then an hour the next evening to get maximum penetration and absorption. Those which have adapted to the slightly acid to neutral sands of the Cross Timbers and some parts of South Texas are more likely to be drought-tolerant. By the way, the sandy soils further west are neutral to basic in reaction like the blacklands.

When you buy a plant *bare root*, it should already have been pruned severely. If it hasn't, cut it back. If you dig up a plant, cut it back two-thirds. If it is a shrub, trim it to a small ball shape. If it is a tree, prune out two-thirds of the branches. Always cut off each branch close to the trunk; otherwise it will sprout several branches where there was just one, and that can ruin the lines and grace of the tree. Water it as you would the container plant. A woody plant, tree, or shrub should be planted bare root only in the winter when it is dormant, and cannot lose water through its leaves.

Once your plants are established, watering should be optional if you have used specimens appropriate to your area. By your area, I don't mean the entire state. Texas, as I have previously mentioned, is varied and extreme. While the magnolia is a Texas native, I would not plant one in the arid Trans-Pecos and expect it to survive. Conversely, some plants, like the cenizo, grow too quickly with excess water, and their branches get brittle. Others, like the bur oak, adjust easily to either situation. Plan your garden with care, and place drought-resistant plants in well-drained spots and water-hungry plants in poorly drained areas.

In a drought it is wise to give your plants an occasional deep watering, if the local water department permits. Plants do die in the wild. You can readily observe damaged leaves or dead branches that were jettisoned when water got too scarce to support the whole plant. To keep a city garden always looking its best, plan to water and prune. The advantage to a native garden is that it looks better on less water than a conventional garden planted with imports.

Julie Ryan

Dry perennial garden with winecup, yarrow, and lantana in front of santolina, coreopsis, and shasta (not native) in background.

Plants for a Perennial Garden

THE PLANTS in this category are those that I would recommend for use in a perennial garden. Most are perennial herbs, but some are actually small shrubs. Some are annuals, and one is a biennial. This was the hardest category to narrow down, because there are so many good possibilities.

This is not surprising when you consider that Texas is considered to be a prairie state—although, as you'll read in the section on prairie, we don't have much authentic virgin prairie still in existence these days. A prairie is not just grasslands; it also abounds with flowers. Most of our flowers like full sun, but a surprising number will take part sun or dappled shade. The bloom times listed are approximate; they will vary with location and weather. However, it is almost always possible to extend the bloom time by providing more water, and giving plants a little relief from the Texas sun.

Another important trick in extending bloom time is to cut off the flower heads before they go to seed. The plant will continue to make flowers as long as it can, in an effort to produce seed. I find that cutting flowers for the house has the same effect.

After a plant has quit blooming and gone to seed, you have several options. You can let the seed scatter. This is good with annuals and biennials that need replanting every year. This is also good if you want to enlarge the space given to a plant. You can always pick the seed and plant it elsewhere, store it for a possible disaster (flood, bulldozer, or child with a toy shovel), or give it to a friend—you can also throw it away.

I cut off the bloom stalk down to 1 or 2 inches. Many plants remain as a groundcover. Those that go dormant in the winter benefit from those 1 to 2 inches of stalk which catch the leaves and give your plant a protective mulch. Nature does not make plants go all winter without a covering. You can water or not. If you do water, your perennial garden will be green and fresh and will bloom from April to frost. If not, spring-blooming plants will turn brown and die, and plants will look good only when it is their time to bloom. Either way, once your garden is established, your plants should not die.

Most people have one of two reactions to wildflowers. They say "They never live, you can't use them" or they say "Just drop them in the ground and they live forever." Of course, neither approach is true. When you first plant them, you need to give them lots of water and care for the first year while their root growth catches up to their top growth. In the wild, a seed will make a rosette, which will remain 3 inches across for a year. All the energy is going into roots. Only after the roots have been growing down deep into the moist earth for a year will the top of the plant make new leaves and bloom. This cautious attitude helps these plants survive our climate. A plant freshly dug or from the nursery has the wrong proportion of top growth to roots, and you have to baby it until the proportions are right. Fertilizer is generally appreciated by wild flowers, with the exception of gaillardia, which gets offensively rambunctious if you give it food. A fertilizer high in phosphorus is good for this group of plants, because it promotes bloom and does not promote such rapid leaf growth that the plant gets out of bounds. With few exceptions I have chosen plants that already grow in sizes and shapes suitable to our gardens.

The advantages to a perennial garden are many. For one thing, you don't have the labor and expense of replanting every year. For another, the variety is not only enjoyable but healthier, because one type of insect cannot ravage your whole garden. Something is blooming all the growing season and something is green and full of promise all winter. The best part of all is weeding. I weed once in early spring before everything gets big. Then I have to weed out the tree seedlings in May. (I live under a pecan, an oak, and an elm.) I weed once more in late fall when I cut off the dead stalks after first frost, but there is generally very little to weed then, because the plants are so thick from May to frost that weeds can't get through. It took only until the second spring for my perennial garden to reach this low-upkeep status.

1. Yarrow
Achillea millefolium
Sally Wasowski

1. **Latin Name** *Achillea millefolium*
    ah-KILL-ee-uh milly-FOLE-ee-um
    Common Name YARROW
    Height 1–2 feet when blooming
    Spacing 1 foot on center
    Bloom Time May–June (4 weeks)
    Range Europe, but naturalized throughout the United States; winter-hardy up to Canada
    Perennial, Evergreen
    Sun to Dappled Shade
    Propagation Seed or root division September–April
    Germination 10 days at 70° F, light needed

Yarrow
Year-Round
Fern

I use this for the 6- to 8-inch-high foliage rather than the blooms; the 3-inch white heads are made up of many tiny flowers, giving the name *millefolium*, which means "thousand flowers." The blooms come at a nice time of year, when there is a little lull between the spring extravaganza and the summer flowers. *Achillea* is very adaptable, taking full sun and drought or moist shady conditions. The foliage stays prettiest all summer if it is given normal watering. If planted to cover large areas, it will occasionally develop bare spots. Dig up a small section in a dense area and simply plug it in, then water. *Achillea* spreads quickly, but the roots are easy to pull out, so it is easy to control.

Commercial varieties are available in pink, which is not as vigorous; *A. filipendulina*, a yellow variety, requires more sun and has coarse foliage. Neither is as well adapted to our area as the naturalized variety.

2. Texas Blue Star
Amsonia ciliata
Benny J. Simpson

3. Wild Columbine
Aquilegia canadensis
Andy Wasowski

2. **Latin Name** *Amsonia ciliata*
      am-SONE-ee-uh see-lee-A-tuh or -AH-tuh
   Common Name TEXAS BLUE STAR
   Height 1–2 feet
   Spacing 1 foot on center
   Bloom Time April, May (2 weeks)
   Range North Carolina to Missouri, North Central Texas to Mexico
   Perennial
   Sun to Part Sun
   Propagation Seed sown in spring or fall, or division of clumps in
      fall or winter

Texas Blue
Star
Big & Blue

Amsonia is clump-forming and very showy because the flower head is large. There are several other amsonias in Texas. All are good. The one shown in the picture is compact and grows well in limestone or sandy loam. The long, thin leaves stay green and attractive until they die back in the fall. This is a long-lasting perennial, the clump getting bigger with age, but not seeding out much. It makes a good cut flower. Cut off the old flower heads after blooming unless you want to collect the seed. This flower needs watering in the summer.

3. **Latin Name** *Aquilegia canadensis*
      ack-wee-LEE-gee-uh kan-uh-DEN-sis
   Common Name WILD COLUMBINE, RED COLUMBINE
   Height 1 foot
   Spacing 9–12 inches on center
   Bloom Time April, May, off and on
   Range Edwards Plateau and eastern United States to Canada
   Perennial
   Dappled Shade or Shade If Part Sun in Early Spring
   Propagation Seed as soon as ripe, spring or fall
      Germination 21–25 days at 70–75° F, light required
      Division of clumps in fall or winter

Wild
Columbine,
Red
Columbine
Made for the
Shade

The graceful columbine remains visually appealing even when it's not in bloom. The foliage dies down at first frost, and new leaves start growing almost immediately. It likes either acid or limy soils, but must have good drainage. If you have clay, be sure to mix several inches of sand or pebbles into the soil. Columbine is wonderful combined with ferns or achillea and rocks under a tree, with slanting sun at bloom time. It also grows well in 6- to 8-inch clay pots. Mine even underwent the Big Freeze in its pot and put out more new leaves the next week.

Longspur Columbine
Columbines for Texas

4. **Latin Name** *Aquilegia longissima*
   ack-wee-LEE-gee-uh lon-JISS-ee-muh
   Common Name LONGSPUR COLUMBINE
   Height 1 foot
   Spacing 9–12 inches on center
   Bloom Time April and occasionally
   Range Trans-Pecos
   Perennial
   Dappled Shade to Shade If Part Sun at Bloom Times
   Propagation Same as for *A. canadensis*

The McKana hybrids are the variety of columbine currently available in our nurseries, but they don't like our hot Texas summers. Our native columbines do better. We have several beautiful yellow varieties. They are not as winter-hardy as the little *A. canadensis* just described, but they are much larger and showier. They grow naturally alongside maidenhair fern in rocky crevices by running water, or in a seep line. Though they like moisture, they must be well drained. *A. longissima* has very long spurs, as you can see by the picture. Each of those blooms is 2 inches wide with spurs up to 6 inches long. From isolated bits of evidence, it appears that these yellow columbines are winter-hardy in North Texas, but if you live north of Dallas–Fort Worth, you might want to keep this one in a pot and take it indoors during the winter.

Butterfly Weed
Attracts Butterflies

5. **Latin Name** *Asclepius tuberosa*
   as-KLEEP-ee-us tuber-ROSE-uh
   Common Name BUTTERFLY WEED
   Height 12–18 inches
   Spacing 1 foot on center
   Bloom Time May and off and on through October
   Range Texas and southeastern United States
   Perennial
   Sun to Dappled Shade
   Propagation Seed or root cuttings
   Fall-sown seed may not show until spring
   Germination 21–28 days at 68–75° F

The monarch butterfly is sometimes called the "milkweed butterfly." *A. tuberosa* is part of the milkweed family and is important as a food for the monarch and for other butterflies, hence its name, "butterfly weed." It has a very stout taproot, so it is not only hard to transplant, it is hard to kill. It takes two or three years to get big enough to display its vibrant blooms, which are clusters 2–3 inches across. Once it is established, it lasts for years, getting thicker and bushier each season. The more branches it gets, the more blooms it gets, so it is showier and blooms longer as it gets older. It tolerates wind and never needs staking. It breaks dormancy and shows new leaves in the spring much later than other plants, so don't give up on it and dig it out. Today, good commercial seed for yellow, orange, or red butterfly weed is available.

4. Longspur Columbine
Aquilegia longissima
Edith Bettinger

5. Butterfly Weed
Asclepius tuberosa
Heard Natural Science Museum

35

**Wild
Hyacinth**
*A Taller
Hyacinth*

6. **Latin Name** *Camassia scilloides*
    kuh-MA-see-uh ske-LOY-dees
   Common Name WILD HYACINTH
   Height 2 feet
   Spacing 4–6 inches on center
   Bloom Time March, April, or May (2 weeks)
   Range North Texas to Canada and Alabama
   Perennial, Bulb
   Sun to Part Sun in Spring
   Propagation Seed (three–four years to bloom from seed)

I use camassia as I would daffodils, massing them where I don't plan to disturb them for years. The foliage is thin and sparse and dies back soon after blooming , so if you want something in that spot all blooming season, interplant with a summer-blooming flower. Lantana or annuals that reseed themselves are best, because planting these will not disturb the bulbs. Plant the small bulbs in late November or early December about 4 inches deep. Most bulbs will take a fair amount of shade as long as they have part sun when it is their time to bloom. Camassia seems to demand more sun than normal, liking full sun the best. Because of their pale blue color and slender growth, they should be planted in a clump to make a nice effect.

**Ox-Eye
Daisy**
*Easier Than
Shasta Daisies*

7. **Latin Name** *Chrysanthemum leucanthemum*
    kruh-SAN-thuh-mum loo-KAN-thuh-mum
   Common Name OX-EYE DAISY
   Height 1 foot
   Spacing 6 inches on center
   Bloom Time April, May, and occasionally thereafter
   Range Northeast corner of Texas and eastern United States
   Perennial
   Sun to Dappled Shade
   Propagation Seed or root division, exceptionally easy
       Germination 10–15 days at 70° F

These 2-inch daisies start blooming in early April and are most flamboyant in the spring. They will continue to bloom a little until frost. They are very healthy and spread rapidly but are easy to control. They make good cut flowers because they last up to seven days. But use flowers with a fresh yellow center; these are as yet unfertilized and will give you a full week's enjoyment. Keep seed heads cut off until fall for a neater appearance and to promote more blooming. Some people recommend cutting back to 4–5 inches for the summer. The leaves will stay green all winter, making a rough winter groundcover.

6. Wild Hyacinth
  Camassia scilloides
  Dr. Geoffrey Stanford

7. Ox-Eye Daisy
  Chrysanthemum leucanthemum
  Sally Wasowski

37

8. Rain Lily
Cooperia drummondii
Sally Wasowski

9. Golden Wave
Coreopsis lanceolata
Julie Ryan

8. **Latin Name**   *Cooperia drummondii*
        coo-PEER-ee-uh druh-MUN-dee-eye
    Common Name   RAIN LILY
    Height   1 foot
    Spacing   4 inches on center
    Bloom Time   September or October
    Range   Texas, northern Mexico to Canada to Louisiana
    Perennial, Evergreen, Bulb
    Sun to Shade
    Propagation   Seed in the fall, division of clumps

Rain Lily
Predictably
Presentable

Cooperia divide rapidly to form neat, attractive clumps of green, grassy foliage. The flowers are 2 inches wide and cover the clumps in fall. The bulbs can be divided and transplanted at any time, even while blooming, with no apparent ill effect. Since the foliage stays green all year and remains the same size, this plant always looks great. My clumps grow in a heavy clay soil, so the bulbs form a mass above ground. If you observe this happening, and you live in an area where the ground freezes, lift the bulbs and store them for the winter. If you have sandy soil, chances are the bulbs will go deep. Plant them from 2 to 4 inches deep, depending on your kind of soil.

---

9. **Latin Name**   *Coreopsis lanceolata*
        ko-ree-OP-sis lan-see-o-LAY-tuh
    Common Name   GOLDEN WAVE
    Height   1–2 feet
    Spacing   1 foot on center
    Bloom Time   May to mid-July
    Range   East and Southeast Texas to New Mexico, Midwest, and
        southeastern United States
    Perennial, Evergreen
    Sun to Dappled Shade
    Propagation   Cuttings, layerings, division of clumps, and seed
        Germination 20–25 days at 55–70° F, light needed

Golden Wave
A Must for
Every
Perennial
Garden

The leaves will look attractive all year as long as you keep them watered and the temperature stays above 10° F. The rosettes spread on woody stems which root at the nodes to make a groundcover. Since coreopsis will seed out enthusiastically if you don't cut off the seed heads after blooming, a little can soon make a lot. Even total neglect on a rental property will not discourage it. However, this growth can be easily contained by cutting off and pulling up unwanted rosettes. Both *C. lanceolata* and *C. grandiflora* have recently entered the nursery trade in Texas. One variety, "Baby Sun," is good to interplant with the above coreopsis, as it blooms two weeks later, giving a solid month of color and cut flowers. *C. tinctoria* is the annual with the dark red spot in the center. I have heard that if watered it will bloom from May until frost. It self-sows very well.

10. White Larkspur
Delphinium virescens
Edith Bettinger

11. Purple Coneflower
Echinacea purpurea
Sally Wasowski

10.   **Latin Name**   *Delphinium virescens*
         dell-FIN-ee-um vie-RES-ins
      Common Name   WHITE LARKSPUR, PRAIRIE LARKSPUR
      Height   1–2 feet, rarely to 5 feet
      Spacing   6 inches on center
      Bloom Time   April–July
      Range   Edwards Plateau north to Canada
      Perennial
      Sun to Part Sun
      Propagation   Seed, spring, or fall
         Germination 8–15 days at 65–75° F

White
Larkspur,
Prairie
Larkspur
*Takes
the Heat*

The beautiful delphiniums in the nursery don't enjoy our hot Texas summers. This delphinium blooms even when it's hot. The plant is skinny and does not branch, so plant a cluster close together to get a good mass of blooms. Each flower on the stalk is 1–1½ inches long. The color is white with a faint bluish tinge, which gets progressively greenish the further west you go in Texas. This faint green cast gives the plant its name: *virescens* means "becoming green." This delphinium can be found in all our soils, sand, black prairie muck, and caliche. The annual bright blue delphinium will grow only in acid sandy soil. Be careful not to plant delphinium where livestock could have access to it, because all parts of the plant have been known to be fatally poisonous to cattle.

---

11.   **Latin Name**   *Echinacea purpurea*
         ek-uh-NAY-see-uh pur-PUR-ee-uh
      Common Name   PURPLE CONEFLOWER
      Height   2–3 feet
      Spacing   1 foot apart
      Bloom Time   May and June (4–6 weeks)
      Range   Northeast Texas to Michigan
      Perennial
      Sun or Part Sun
      Propagation   Seed spring or fall or division of clumps
         Germination 10–20 days at 70–75° F

Purple
Coneflower
*Flamboyant
Hot Pink*

This is the coneflower I would use in my garden. It has had some breeding to make it shorter, with more and larger flowers. The bright pink is very colorful. It does great in our limy soils and is drought-resistant with no supplemental watering in Dallas. It is easily found in seed racks and is fairly common in area flower gardens. *E. angustifolia* is the species most commonly found wild here. My grandmother called it "black sampson." It grows from the Edwards Plateau north to Canada. It is taller and paler, and the petals droop. Other native varieties range in color from white to lavender, dark red, and dark purple—very pretty. They all make good cut flowers. If you don't want the seeds, cut off the spent blooms. The seed heads are painfully prickly.

12. Claret Cup Cactus
Echinocereus triglochidiatus
Harold Laughlin

13. Blue Boneset
Eupatorium coelestinum
Heard Natural Science Museum

12. **Latin Name**   *Echinocereus triglochidiatus* var. *melanacanthus*
ee-ki-no-SEER-ee-us tri-glo-ky-dee-A-tus variety mel-an-uh-CAN-thus
Common Name   CLARET CUP CACTUS
Height   1 foot
Spacing   2 feet on center
Bloom Time   May, June
Range   Colorado to Mexico
Perennial, Evergreen
Sun to Shade, If Part Sun When Blooming
Propagation   Seed spring or fall

Claret Cup
Cactus
*Cold-Weather
Cactus*

Cacti are in high demand, but most are not winter-hardy in North Texas. This one is. Its 2- to 3-inch blooms range in color from the purple illustrated (the color of claret) to hot pink to scarlet. The succulent stems, not over a foot long and 2–3 inches wide, are densely covered with spines. Because these stems are fleshy, like those of most cacti, it does best on sand or limestone soils, because it can easily rot if it gets too wet. If you live on the blacklands, dig in lots of sand and plant it on a slope or a berm, perhaps with a rock above to divert water away from its base. Even so, you might lose it in a wet spring. It grows very well in a clay pot. The soil can be pure sand with regular feedings dissolved in the waterings, or it can be a sand and mulch mixture. Do not use peat or potting soil, or it could rot out after a soaking rain. The fruits are very spiny, but as they ripen to a bright red, the spines fall away.

---

13. **Latin Name**   *Eupatorium coelestinum*
you-pah-TORE-ee-um see-LES-tee-num
Common Name   BLUE BONESET, FOAMFLOWER
Height   2 feet
Spacing   1–3 feet on center
Bloom Time   Late July to November
Range   New Jersey to Michigan to Texas
Perennial
Sun to Dappled Shade
Propagation   Division of roots or seed

Blue
Boneset,
Foamflower
*Ageratum
Look-Alike*

I find this plant amazing. One spring, I pulled up a seedling in sandy acid soil by a lake edge and planted it in the black soil where my sprinkler system drains. By summer, it was a thick, luxurious mass occupying one square foot of my garden. It bloomed all fall in a great mass of purple. It had gone from full sun to dappled shade, from acid to alkaline. It throve. The next spring I pulled a hunk of root out and split it and planted it in a poorly drained area of black gumbo, in full sun, with reflected heat on two sides. By mid-summer, the ground was so dry it was cracking. By fall, the *Eupatorium* looked like it had been growing there forever and produced a long-lasting display. Though it spreads quickly, the roots are easy to remove, so it is a cinch to control. The lavender blooms look wonderful with lantana or a mass of chrysanthemums.

43

14. **Latin Name** *Eustoma grandiflorum*
you-STO-muh gran-dee-FLORE-um

Texas Bluebell, Purple Prairie Gentian
A Long-Lasting Cut Flower

Common Name TEXAS BLUEBELL, PURPLE PRAIRIE GENTIAN
Height 1–2 feet
Spacing 1 foot on center
Bloom Time Mid-June to August
Range Nebraska, Colorado, Texas, New Mexico
Annual
Sun
Propagation Seed, fall best
Germination 10–14 days at 70° F

We used to have more of these by our roadsides. But they're such wonderful flowers that many people picked them in bunches, not leaving many to form seeds for reproduction. The flowers are 2–3 inches wide and exceptionally pretty, usually lavender blue, but also pink, blue, white, or yellow. The Japanese are breeding them and calling them "lisianthus." The seed (fine as dust and difficult to propagate) is now becoming available. Everett E. Janne of Texas A&M has had excellent results broadcasting the seed onto flats filled with moist peat and perlite in early January in the greenhouse. Then, after gradually moving them up to 3-inch containers, he plants them in the garden as soon as the danger of frost is over. Some will even bloom in the container. In the wild, the seed usually germinates in the spring, sometimes in the fall, and winters-over before blooming the next summer. Self-sowing is somewhat erratic. This would be an excellent plant for nurseries to sell.

---

15. **Latin Name** *Habranthus texanus*
hah-BRAN-thus tex-A-nus

Copper Lily
Autumn Delight

Common Name COPPER LILY
Height 1 foot
Spacing 6 inches on center
Bloom Time September
Range East Texas west to the Edwards Plateau and south along the coast
Perennial Bulb
Sun to Dappled Shade
Propagation Division of clumps, seed

These little lilies are beautiful massed in the foreground of any garden. They grow naturally in swampy, sunny places, but they do well on dry land and bloom in the shade like their cousins, the *Cooperia*. If you live north of Austin, work a lot of sand into the soil to lighten it, so that you can plant them 4–6 inches deep to give them some protection from the cold. If your soil is very thin, try planting them as deeply as you can and giving them a top mulch. If you live in an area where the ground routinely freezes, withhold water after blooming to force them into dormancy, and dig and store them at 60° F. Otherwise, enjoy them all year, for they stay green all winter in mild climates.

14. Texas Bluebell
Eustoma grandiflorum
Dr. Geoffrey Stanford

45

15. Copper Lily
Habranthus texanus
Benny J. Simpson

**Red
Yucca**
*Graceful
Accent*

16. **Latin Name**   *Hesperaloe parviflora*
       hes-per-A-loh-ee par-vee-FLORE-uh
    Common Name   RED YUCCA
    Height   Flowers 6 feet, leaves 2–3 feet
    Spacing   3 feet on center
    Bloom Time   May, June
    Range   Western Edwards Plateau
    Perennial, Evergreen
    Sun to Dappled Shade
    Propagation   Seed or division of root stock

Hesperaloe looks best as an accent plant in a rock garden, with yucca, *Leucophyllum frutescens* (cenizo or Texas sage), santolina, junipers, and so forth. The foliage is a soft blue-green, the flowers shrimp-pink. When not in bloom, the plant still offers great eye-appeal; its graceful leaves are very attractive all year round. It reaches maximum size in three to five years. Though it is extremely drought-resistant, it must have a full year of care and watering to get well established. This plant is used in landscapes all over the world. It is usually readily available in nurseries.

**Texas Star
Hibiscus**
*True
Texan?*

17. **Latin Name**   *Hibiscus coccineus*
       hi-BIS-kus kox-SIN-ee-us
    Common Name   TEXAS STAR HIBISCUS
    Height   6 feet
    Spacing   3 feet on center
    Bloom Time   June to October
    Range   Rare in the Big Thicket, southern Georgia, and Florida
    Perennial
    Sun
    Propagation   Seed or root cuttings

It is ironic that this hibiscus is the one called "Texas star," because it is possible that it isn't native to Texas at all, and that the specimens in the Big Thicket have naturalized there. These huge, beautiful flowers are a pleasure around a pool area because they bloom the whole warm season. Strong smooth stalks are sent up each spring from a base, more stalks each year, more blooms each year. Hibiscus is naturally a swamp plant, so give it plenty of water, especially in August and September, or it will stop blooming and die back to its roots prematurely. I have used this plant successfully in an 18-inch pot with an annual planted around the base. Some other hibiscus (bona fide Texans) are *H. moscheutos*, which has 6–8-inch flowers, and *H. cardiophyllus*, which is 3 feet high and has 3-inch red flowers. Both these hibiscus have heart-shaped leaves. *H. militaris*, which has 5–6-inch pale pink or white flowers with a maroon throat, has halberd-shaped leaves. All hibiscus may have heart-shaped leaves when young. All of these are winter-hardy in Texas.

16. Red Yucca
Hesperaloe parviflora
Julie Ryan

17. Texas Star Hibiscus
Hibiscus coccineus
Harold Laughlin

47

18. Spider Lily
Hymenocallis liriosme
Edith Bettinger

19. Red Gilia
Ipomopsis rubra
Andy Wasowski

48

18. **Latin Name** *Hymenocallis liriosme*
       hi-me-no-KAL-is lih-ree-OZE-me
    Common Name SPIDER LILY
    Height 2 feet
    Spacing 1 foot on center
    Bloom Time April, May (2 weeks)
    Range Wet places in Texas north to Arkansas, Oklahoma
    Perennial Bulb
    Sun to Part Sun
    Propagation Division of clumps

Spider
Lily
Spectacular

These elegant flowers are 4–6 inches wide. Their main requirement is lots of water in the spring. I planted mine near a hydrant. *H. caroliniana* of the southeastern United States is very similar. In climates north of Denton, dig the bulbs and store in the house over the winter. It is best not to plant these bulbs in a raised bed, both because of the danger of freezing and because it is harder to get them moist enough that way. They like only about an inch of soil on their tops, which is not much protection from cold or the summer sun. If mine were not covered with an evergreen groundcover, I would keep them mulched. The blooms make the trouble worthwhile. They start opening about four or five o'clock in the afternoon. You can watch them unfurl. They are wonderfully fragrant, and when you smell them you get golden pollen all over your face. They multiply and transplant well, lasting for years with the proper care.

---

19. **Latin Name** *Ipomopsis rubra*
       eye-po-MOP-sis RUBE-bruh
    Common Name RED GILIA, STANDING CYPRESS
    Height 2–6 feet
    Spacing 6 inches on center
    Bloom Time May to July (4–6 weeks)
    Range Central Texas to eastern United States
    Biennial
    Sun to Dappled Shade
    Propagation Seed sown in the fall
       Germination 10–15 days at 55–65° F

Red Gilia,
Standing
Cypress
*Tiny Red
Trumpets*

Start from seed. In the first year of growth there will be a ferny rosette. The second year will produce the flower. The blooms start at the top of the spike. When the spike has bloomed out, cut it off; new blooming spikes will develop. In this way you can get the plant to bloom for eight to ten weeks. The best way to have this flower every year is to choose an area in your garden at least 2 feet by 2 feet. Plant the seed two consecutive years to ensure that you always have rosettes and bloom stalks. Let the blooms seed out every year. If rosettes begin where you do not want them, be sure to transplant them the first year before vertical growth has begun. The root is very deep, and it is almost impossible to get enough of it for a good transplant after the plant is very big.

49

20. Louisiana Iris
Iris brevicaulis
Andy Wasowski

21. Texas Lantana
Lantana horrida
Julie Ryan

20.   **Latin Name**   *Iris brevicaulis*
            EYE-ris bre-vee-KAW-lis
       Common Name   LOUISIANA IRIS
       Height   1½–2 feet
       Spacing   1 foot on center
       Bloom Time   May (10 days)
       Range   Alabama to Texas to Kansas to Ohio
       Perennial, Evergreen
       Sun to Dappled Shade
       Propagation   Seed as soon as ripe, division of clumps

Louisiana
Iris
Well-Bred

I. brevicaulis is just one of the Louisiana iris. Several different have been hybridized, so that the bloom stalks and foliage range from 1 to 5 feet tall and the flowers may be 3 to 7 inches wide. The colors run the gamut of the rainbow, appropriately, since *Iris* means "rainbow." In summer these iris need a mulch or the shade of other plants to protect the rhizomes. The leaves stay green all summer on most species if they receive water about once a week. Otherwise they die back and leaf out again in the fall. They look and bloom better with a side-dressing of azalea food spring and fall. This is hardly consistent with the scope of the book, but these iris are so lovely I felt that the general public should be more aware of them.

---

21.   **Latin Name**   *Lantana horrida*
            lan-TAN-uh HOR-ee-duh
       Common Name   TEXAS LANTANA, ORANGE LANTANA
       Height   18 inches to 3 feet
       Spacing   3 feet on center
       Bloom Time   Late May until frost
       Range   Texas except the Panhandle
       Perennial
       Sun to Part Sun
       Propagation   Seed, layering, root division, spring cuttings
            Germination 6–8 weeks (*or longer*) at 70–75° F

Texas
Lantana,
Orange
Lantana
*Survives Our
Worst Winters*

This lantana is *horrida* because whoever named it hated the pungent smell of its leaves. I love it! *L. camara* var. *mista* (West Indian lantana), which has naturalized in much of Texas, has larger leaves but otherwise looks the same. *L. macropoda* has pink and yellow flowers. I got my lantana when a friend's mother spaded up a length of root and stem and simply handed it to me. That was in July, not a good time to transplant, yet it has flourished through four moves, two 5° F winters, a swampy spring, and one torrid summer when it got no water. Now it is even blooming profusely in dappled shade, although it prefers full sun. Lantana will make a tall groundcover if you let it spread. If you want to curb yours, trim it back to 2 inches every winter after first frost when it dies back. If a branch has rooted, cut it loose on either side. Dig it up and transplant it in February or March. I like lantana interplanted with spring bulbs, because it starts to bloom just as the bulb leaves are ready to be cut.

Gayfeather, Blazing Star
Very Showy

22. **Latin Name** *Liatris* spp.
       lye-A-tris
     Common Name GAYFEATHER, BLAZING STAR
     Height 2 feet, usually
     Spacing 1 foot to 18 inches on center
     Bloom Time September, October (1 month)
     Range Great Plains states
     Perennial
     Sun to Part Sun
     Propagation Division of corms, soft stem cuttings, or seed
       Germination 20–25 days (varies a lot) at 55–75° F
       Freezing 3 weeks sometimes aids germination

There are many varieties of liatris in Texas, *L. punctata* (1–3 feet) and *L. pycnostachya* (2–5 feet) being the most drought-tolerant. *L. spicata*, native to the eastern United States and most often found in the nursery trade, grows well in Texas, but is not native here. Liatris has one failing—sometimes its bloom stalks flop over. The way to prevent this is to keep the plant dry in July and August to strengthen the stems. In a garden where it gets regular watering and some fertilizer, the blooming spikes get so big and showy that they are too heavy for the plant to hold up. In these conditions, I position the liatris behind a rock or on the edge of a retaining wall so that it looks good spilling over. After it blooms, cut the stalks to the ground. New stalks will grow the next spring.

Cardinal Flower
Brilliant Color for Places Shady

23. **Latin Name** *Lobelia cardinalis*
       low-BEE-lee-uh card-ee-NAL-is
     Common Name CARDINAL FLOWER
     Height 1 to 4 feet
     Spacing 1 foot on center
     Bloom Time August to October
     Range Eastern half of United States and Canada
     Perennial
     Dappled Shade to Part Sun
     Propagation Seed, root division, layering
       Germination 15–20 days at 70° F

L. cardinalis belongs in a shady, well-watered place with columbine and maidenhair fern, perhaps in front of your azaleas or under your eastern dogwood, if you have such acid-loving, water-guzzling plants already in your yard. It has made the adjustment to alkaline soils, even growing right out of limestone crevices on the edge of a stream. However, it is not a robust plant or a long-lived perennial. To keep cardinal flower in your yard, do a little propagation each year. Bury a stem or two still attached to the plant. You can hold it down with a rock. New plants will sprout from the leaf nodes. This is called layering. In very early spring or early fall, dig up some of the plants on the edge of an old clump and transplant them. Cardinal flower blooms in the fall when the hummingbirds migrate through Texas on their way south—a benefit to both. The hummingbirds get nectar and the flower gets pollinated. The seed are incredibly tiny.

22. Gayfeather
Liatris spp.
Julie Ryan

23. Cardinal Flower
Lobelia cardinalis
Heard Natural
Science Museum

24. **Latin Name** *Machaeranthera tanacetifolia*
mack-uh-RAN-the-rah tan-uh-see-tee-FO-lee-uh

Tahoka Daisy, Tansy Aster
Purple Daisies All Summer

Common Name TAHOKA DAISY, TANSY ASTER
Height 1–2 feet
Spacing 1 foot on center
Bloom Time May to October
Range Trans-Pecos south to central Mexico and north to Alberta, Canada
Annual
Sun to Part Sun
Propagation Seed, fall-sown or chilled two weeks in the refrigerator
Germination 25–30 days at 70° F

The flowers are 2 inches or more across. The leaves are so finely divided that they appear almost ferny, but they are sticky to the touch. Under good conditions (and Tahoka daisy is not very picky about what conditions are good) the leaves are so dense that they form a 1-foot mound, which is then covered with the flowers. The flowers are usually the lavender blue shown in the picture, but they are occasionally a very pale blue or a violet pink. They bloom all summer, no matter how hot it gets. Because of this extravagance of bloom, and the neat habit of growth, Tahoka daisy has been extensively cultivated. Unfortunately, it is seen very rarely in this area. It would be an excellent annual bedding plant for our nurseries to carry. It likes sun and well-drained soil.

---

25. **Latin Name** *Malvaviscus drummondii*
mal-vuh-VISK-us druh-MUN-dee-eye

Turk's Cap
Attracts Hummingbirds

Common Name TURK'S CAP
Height 2½–9 feet
Spacing 2–5 feet on center
Bloom Time May to frost
Range Southeastern United States to Edwards Plateau
Perennial
Part Sun to Dappled Shade
Propagation Softwood cutting, seed, and division of clumps

Turk's cap grows to 5 feet by 9 feet, is evergreen, and blooms all year along the Gulf Coast in places where frost is a rarity. There, they also have two tropical varieties with larger flowers. In Dallas–Fort Worth, it goes dormant for the winter and rarely gets over 3 feet high by 3 feet wide. The soft, heart-shaped leaves and little red flowers are a subtle spot of color all the blooming season. And, like the *Anisacanthus*, it may well lure a hummingbird to stay in your yard all summer. It dies back after first frost and looks much better if you cut off the old stalks. It is not particular as to soil or water. The fruits are 1 inch long and bright red. Not only are they visually attractive, but they provide food for many birds.

24. Tahoka Daisy
Machaeranthera tanacetifolia
Edith Bettinger

25. Turk's Cap
Malvaviscus drummondii
Edith Bettinger

26. Blackfoot Daisy
Melampodium cinereum
Sally Wasowski

27. Walking Stick Cholla
Opuntia imbricata
Julie Ryan

26. **Latin Name** *Melampodium cinereum*
 mel-lam-PODE-ee-um sin-ear-RE-um
 Common Name BLACKFOOT DAISY, MOUNTAIN DAISY
 Height 1 foot
 Spacing 9 feet on center
 Bloom Time April to frost
 Range Limestone areas of Arkansas to Colorado to Texas
 Perennial
 Sun to Dappled Shade
 Propagation Fall-sown seed

Blackfoot
Daisy,
Mountain
Daisy
*Put It
Anywhere*

This little beauty will transplant well, even in full bloom. It loves full sun, but will also bloom profusely in dappled shade, as long as it is not suffocated by another plant. It is not fussy about damp or dry soil. This tidy little plant is covered with white flowers all spring, summer, and fall. It is low-growing, so display it prominently along walkways and right up front in your garden. You may notice that it seems to have disappeared in the winter. But don't worry—it will reliably return in the spring and be blooming by the time the bluebonnets are.

27. **Latin Name** *Opuntia imbricata*
 o-PUN-she-uh im-bree-KAY-tuh
 Common Name WALKING STICK CHOLLA (CHOY-yuh)
 Height 1–6 feet
 Spacing 2–4 feet on center
 Bloom Time April and June
 Range Trans-Pecos north to Kansas
 Perennial
 Sun to Part Sun
 Propagation Plant pad

Walking
Stick
Cholla
High & Dry

There are few hardy cacti in North Central Texas, so if you are a cactus fan, this one might be a good addition to your garden. It has a short, woody trunk and a branching pattern which is very different from our prickly pear, and the 3-inch purple flowers are gorgeous. The fruits are yellow and fleshy, about 1 inch long. Cacti like a sandy or limestone situation, good drainage being the important thing. This one is very slow-growing. It can be started from an elbow or L-shaped cutting. Put one side in the ground and firm the soil over it and leave the other above ground. Do this in late spring or summer when it will be dry and won't rot.

28. Prickly Pear
Opuntia phaeacantha
Steve Runnels, Dallas Museum of Natural History (DMNH)

29. Pavonia
Pavonia lasiopetala
Julie Ryan

28. **Latin Name** *Opuntia phaeacantha*
o-PUN-she-uh fay-uh-CAN-thah
Common Name TEXAS PRICKLY PEAR
Height 1–3 feet
Spacing 2 feet on center
Bloom Time April, May
Range Central Texas
Perennial
Sun to Dappled Shade
Propagation Pad or seed

Texas Prickly Pear Doesn't Need a Desert

There are several species of prickly pear; this one is winter-hardy in all of North Central Texas, but it seems to be at its northern limit here and rarely gets over 1 foot tall. It does not seem to be very particular as to soil, and even does fine in well-watered yards. If you want to grow one in a patio pot, make sure it is not in a traffic area. The yellow flowers are 3–4 inches across. Propagation is usually from pads or "pears." Break one off, let it dry in a shady place until calloused, and then root it in sand. When grown from seed, it looks like a skinny green finger when it first comes up.

29. **Latin Name** *Pavonia lasiopetala*
puh-VO-nee-uh lay-zee-o-PET-uh-luh
Common Name PAVONIA
Height 2–5 feet, shorter in North Texas
Spacing 4 feet on center
Bloom Time May until frost
Range Southwest Texas and Mexico
Perennial
Sun to Dappled Shade
Propagation Seed, hardwood or softwood cuttings

Pavonia One of the Best

This shrubby little plant is a delight. The satiny pink hibiscus-like blossoms are 1½ inches across and are scattered all over the plant every day. They close up at night. Cut back the woody stems each winter to keep the plant thick and trim. That's all you have to do for it all year. Though it is drought-resistant, it can take lots of water. However, it does not like sand and grows best out of limestone or black prairie soil. Denton is probably its northernmost limit. If I lived north of there I would grow it in a pot and bring it in every winter, or buy a gallon-sized plant each year. It makes an excellent patio pot plant.

30. Wild Foxglove
Penstemon cobaea
Julie Ryan

31. Scarlet Penstemon
Penstemon murrayanus
Dr. Geoffrey Stanford

30. **Latin Name** *Penstemon cobaea*
        PEN-stuh-mun KO-bee-uh or ko-BEE-uh
    Common Name WILD FOXGLOVE, BEARD TONGUE, CANTERBURY
        BELLS
    Height 2 feet
    Spacing 1 foot on center
    Bloom Time April, May (2–3 weeks)
    Range Texas Gulf Coast north and west to Nebraska
    Perennial
    Sun to Part Sun
    Propagation Seed or division of root stock

Wild
Foxglove,
Beard Tongue,
Canterbury
Bells
Dramatic

The flower stalks are over a foot high, with individual blooms being 3 inches long. The colors range from roses and lavenders to white, the markings in the throat being a deeper, contrasting hue. When it is not blooming, the plant is a rosette, 3 or 4 inches wide, and green all winter. It will grow in limestone or sand or black clay. If in full sun, it needs occasional watering during the summer to keep its foliage attractive. Cut down the bloom stalks right after blooming unless you want the seed. You can have a very showy planting from seed the second spring.

31. **Latin Name** *Penstemon murrayanus*
        PEN-stuh-mun mur-ee-ANE-us
    Common Name SCARLET PENSTEMON
    Height 2–3 feet
    Spacing 1 foot on center
    Bloom Time April to July
    Range East Texas to North Central Texas
    Perennial
    Sun to Part Sun
    Propagation Fall-sown seed, chill seed before sowing in spring

Scarlet
Penstemon
*Hot-Weather
Penstemon*

This penstemon looks very similar to *P. havardii*, which is supposed to bloom from June to October in the Trans-Pecos. Both scarlet penstemons have distinctive rounded leaves that literally surround the stem. I have seen the East Texas penstemon in bloom later than it should be in August, and the West Texas variety blooming earlier than normal in April. Neither is listed for North Central Texas or is supposed to bloom on limestone, but I have seen a plant that looks just like it blooming out of limestone in Duncanville. It's a handsome plant even when not in bloom, and its red blossoms attract hummingbirds. This plant is very straight and slim, and looks best in clumps of five or more. It goes dormant in the winter. Cut off the stalk after first frost.

Louisiana Phlox, Wild Blue Phlox
Long Spring Bloomer

32. **Latin Name**   *Phlox divaricata*
    FLOCKS dye-ver-ee-KAY-tuh
    Common Name   LOUISIANA PHLOX, WILD BLUE PHLOX
    Height   1 foot
    Spacing   1 foot on center
    Bloom Time   March and April
    Range   East Texas to western Florida north to South Dakota
    Perennial, Semi-Evergreen
    Sun to Dappled Shade
    Propagation   Seed or division of clumps or cuttings in early summer

The true color range of this flower is white to lavender to purple. This phlox combines well with all the spring-blooming bulbs. Best of all, the small, dark leaves make low attractive clumps, so that it looks appealing all year and is suitable for bordering your garden. I know this phlox will go two months in the summer without water, but I don't know if it will survive a ground-cracking drought. A more drought-resistant perennial phlox is *P. mesoleuca*, which has a white eye in the center of each bloom. It occurs naturally in the Trans-Pecos, blooming all summer. Its winter-hardiness further north is unknown.

P. divaricata is readily available in area nurseries.

Drummond's Phlox
Likes Sand

33. **Latin Name**   *Phlox drummondii*
    FLOCKS druh-MUN-dee-eye
    Common Name   DRUMMOND'S PHLOX
    Height   6 inches
    Spacing   6 inches on center
    Bloom Time   April and May
    Range   East Central Texas
    Annual
    Sun
    Propagation   Seed
    Germination 10–15 days at 55–65° F

This phlox will grow in well-prepared black soil, but it will not self-sow freely as it will in sand, so you will have to reseed or replant every year. As you can see from the picture, it is a delightful little thing, and it is available in our nurseries in the spring. It was taken to England in 1834 by Thomas Drummond. Since then it has been hybridized, and seed is widely available. In sandy places, it forms a carpet of colors. A red variety is available from California. The plant dies after going to seed, so you need to plant it with lantana or pavonia, both of which are bare in the early spring, allowing the phlox to bloom and go to seed, with the lantana and pavonia expanding and blooming from late May until frost, filling the space the phlox left.

32. Louisiana Phlox
Phlox divaricata
Dr. Geoffrey Stanford

33. Drummond's Phlox
Phlox drummondii
Harold Laughlin

34. Lionheart (Fall)
Physostegia praemorsa
Harold Laughlin

35. Lionheart (Spring)
Physostegia pulchella
Dr. Geoffrey Stanford

64

34. **Latin Name**   *Physostegia praemorsa*
     fie-so-STEE-gee-uh pree-MORE-suh
    Common Name   LIONHEART, FALSE DRAGON-HEAD, OBEDIENT PLANT
    Height   1–2 feet
    Spacing   1 foot on center
    Bloom Time   August to October (3–4 weeks)
    Range   North Central Texas, Louisiana to New Mexico, Guadalupe Mts.
    Perennial
    Sun to Dappled Shade
    Propagation   Seed or division of clumps
     Germination 20–25 days at 70–75° F

Lionheart (Fall), False Dragon-Head, Obedient Plant *Autumn Pastel*

Of all the physostegias, this is my personal favorite. It is the shortest and most drought-tolerant, and its pale pink to lavender color is a refreshing contrast among all the bright yellow flowers that are so typical of autumn. The individual bloom stalks are 4 to 6 inches long, so they make a dramatic spot of color in your garden. The plants also yield excellent cut flowers, long-lasting and easy to arrange. The plants are clump-forming, so each year they make a more splendid display. If your clump spreads too far, use a sharp spade to cut around the plant where you want the boundaries to be. This way you won't disturb the roots you want to keep. Then pull out the unwanted roots. These will transplant easily if you want to start another colony.

35. **Latin Name**   *Physostegia pulchella*
     fie-so-STEE-gee-uh pull-KELL-uh
    Common Name   LIONHEART, FALSE DRAGON-HEAD, OBEDIENT PLANT
    Height   1–2 feet (taller if kept very moist)
    Spacing   1 foot on center
    Bloom Time   April to June
    Range   Eastern third of Texas
    Perennial
    Sun to Dappled Shade
    Propagation   Seed or division of clumps
     Germination 20–25 days at 70–75° F

Lionheart (Spring), False Dragon-Head, Obedient Plant *Colorful Colonies*

We have several physostegias. Looking very similar to the photo, but more purple than hot pink, is *P. angustifolia*, which is winter-hardy all the way up to Illinois. *P. digitalis*, slightly paler, is winter-hardy as far north as Oklahoma. All of these are spring-blooming physostegias and are equally usable. These plants grow naturally in swampy places, but they will tolerate conditions as dry as those in Dallas. They form thick colonies which are striking when in bloom. They can be invasive, but they are easy to control. The roots you dig out will transplant easily. The name "obedient plant" denotes a peculiar characteristic: if you move one of the flowers on the stem, it will stay exactly where you put it. For this reason, as well as its attractiveness, *Physostegia* is ideal in floral arrangements.

36. Mexican Hat
  Ratibida columnaris
  Benny J. Simpson

37. Black-Eyed Susan
  Rudbeckia hirta
  Harold Laughlin

36. **Latin Name** *Ratibida columnaris*
    ruh-TIB-uh-duh kol-um-NARE-is
    Common Name MEXICAN HAT
    Height 2–3 feet
    Spacing 1 foot on center
    Bloom Time June to frost
    Range North Dakota to Mexico
    Perennial
    Sun to Dappled Shade
    Propagation Seed sown spring or fall or division of clumps

Mexican Hat
Blooms All Summer

The 1–2-inch flowers are pure yellow to pure chocolate, usually red-brown in the center and yellow on the edges. The blooms are not dense enough to be suitable for a mass planting, but ratibida is delightful scattered in your perennial garden or in a pot, because the foliage is light, airy, and graceful, getting denser each year. It makes a good summer-time cut flower display, combining well in texture and color with the other summer-blooming flowers mentioned in this book. Ratibida is drought-resistant, but doesn't mind being in a well-watered yard. It blooms the second year from seed, the first year giving all its attention to root growth. *R. peduncularis*, the annual, is similar in appearance. Both ratibidas seed out freely, so be sure to weed out seedlings, or they can overtake your garden. Cut to the ground after frost.

37. **Latin Name** *Rudbeckia hirta*
    rud-BECK-ee-uh HEER-tuh
    Common Name BLACK-EYED SUSAN
    Height 1–2 feet
    Spacing 1 foot on center
    Bloom Time June through September
    Range Eastern half of North America
    Annual or Short-Lived Perennial
    Sun to Part Sun
    Propagation Fall- or spring-sown seed
    Germination 5–10 days at 70–75° F

Black-Eyed Susan
Summer Color

Rudbeckia blooms well on the edge of a wood or in dappled shade. But it tends to get mildewed there, so make sure it gets enough sun to dry the leaves. If it gets a lot of sun, make sure it gets plenty of water. In other words, treat it as you would zinnias. Gloriosa daisy is a cultivated perennial version that deserves to be used more often in our area. I have seen it bloom from June to August, and then again from October to frost. Blooms are 3 inches across. It self-sows fairly well, but sometimes where you least expect it. Move the rosettes to the *Rudbeckia* spot in the fall or early spring. You can tell them from most of the other rosettes, because the leaves are very soft and furry.

38. Scarlet Sage
Salvia coccinea
Edith Bettinger

39. Mealy Blue Sage
Salvia farinacea
Sally Wasowski

38. **Latin Name** *Salvia coccinea*
    SAL-vee-uh cock-SIN-ee-uh
    Common Name SCARLET SAGE, TROPICAL SAGE
    Height 1–2 feet
    Spacing 1 foot on center
    Bloom Time April to June and August to November
    Range South Carolina to eastern half of Texas
    Perennial
    Part Sun to Dappled Shade
    Propagation Seed or cuttings
    Germination 12–15 days at 70° F, light required

Scarlet Sage, Tropical Sage
Lures Hummingbirds & Butterflies

Though its natural habitat is sand, this salvia grows well on limestone and in blacklands soil, but it will not seed as well there. It is fairly drought-resistant, but should get some water during the hottest part of the summer. It will grow in full sun, but only if adequately watered. *Salvia* is in the mint family. It is winter-hardy, freezing back to roots in a hard winter, but returning in spring. It greatly resembles the Brazilian *S. splendens*, the well-known annual of the nursery trade.

---

39. **Latin Name** *Salvia farinacea*
    SAL-vee-uh fair-uh-NAY-cee-uh
    Common Name MEALY BLUE SAGE
    Height 2–3 feet
    Spacing 1–2 feet on center
    Bloom Time April to November (sometimes in July)
    Range Most of Texas
    Perennial
    Sun to Part Sun
    Propagation Seed or cuttings
    Germination 12–15 days at 70° F

Mealy Blue Sage
Summertime Blues

This is the most usable of the native blue sages, because of its smaller size and its ability to make an attractive mass of color. The leaves have a grayish cast in summer, which makes a good contrast in a lush green display, or looks right at home in a desert garden. It makes an excellent accent plant for a rock garden. It loves limestone and black clay soils. "Blue Bedder" is a commercial variety of *S. farinacea* that can be found in better local nurseries, or through seed catalogs. It is a bright, clear blue. A very short blue salvia is *S. texana*, a neat mound 8–12 inches tall, covered with purplish blue flowers with white throats, and pleasingly fragrant. It blooms from March to October in Central and West Texas.

Cherry Sage, Autumn Sage
Easy & Rewarding

40. **Latin Name** *Salvia greggii*
    SAL-vee-uh GREG-ee-eye
    Common Name   CHERRY SAGE, AUTUMN SAGE
    Height   2–3 feet
    Spacing   2 feet on center
    Bloom Time   April to frost, off and on
    Range   Central, South, and West Texas
    Perennial
    Sun, Part Sun, Dappled Shade
    Propagation   Seed, softwood cuttings in the spring, or hardwood cuttings in the winter

This salvia is shrubby. Unpruned, it is thin and graceful. With pruning, it can look like a neat mound up to 2 feet high and broad. *S. greggii* comes in red, white, or pink. A blue shrubby salvia is *S. lycioides*. All of these salvias are winter-hardy, extremely drought-resistant, and long-lived. By now, you have probably figured out that any salvia you might find is going to be a good garden plant. Use any of them as an accent plant in a small garden, or mass them for color in a larger area. The plants are covered with 1-inch blossoms in April and October and have less conspicuous color during the summer. Pick a leaf and rub it between your fingers. It gives off a wonderful smell.

Goldenrod
Not Guilty

41. **Latin Name** *Solidago* spp.
    sol-uh-DAY-go species
    Common Name   GOLDENROD
    Height   2–3 feet
    Spacing   1 foot on center
    Bloom Time   October (1 week)
    Range   Edwards Plateau to Canada
    Perennial
    Sun to Dappled Shade
    Propagation   Seed sown in spring or fall, root division

Solidago has been much maligned as a cause of hayfever; it is not wind-pollinated. Rather, it is a source of nectar for bees and butterflies and has a delightful fragrance. Solidago is glorious when in bloom. It is drought-resistant and tolerant of shade. The clumps get bigger each year, providing a bigger and better show. If it gets lots of water or if it sits in heavy shade and has to reach toward the sun, it might get up to 5 feet tall, but it will still bloom. Cut to 2 inches after flowering. The leaves will remain green and low to the ground all winter. I have not mentioned a particular species, because solidagos are very hard to classify. If you are gathering your own seed, pick out the prettiest one in your area and don't worry about it if you can't exactly identify which one it is. Be aware that some sucker badly.

40. Cherry Sage
Salvia greggii
Julie Ryan

41. Goldenrod
Solidago spp.
Dr. Geoffrey Stanford

Greenthread, False Golden Wave
Leaves Are Green Threads

42. **Latin Name** *Thelesperma filifolium*
    thell-iss-SPERM-uh fill-ee-FOLE-ee-um
    Common Name GREENTHREAD, FALSE GOLDEN WAVE
    Height 1 foot
    Spacing 6 inches on center
    Bloom Time May to September
    Range Central Texas
    Annual
    Sun to Part Sun
    Propagation Seed, fall best

Thelesperma looks so much like coreopsis that it is difficult to tell the flowers apart. The main difference is that the leaves in thelesperma are thin and delicate and not evergreen. The other difference is that thelesperma is more at home on pure limestone. *T. simplicifolium* is the perennial species that I would recommend; it grows up to 2 feet tall, but otherwise looks very similar to the thelesperma pictured. If you use the annual, you will have to transplant seedlings in the fall or early spring to get them placed exactly where you want. It is easier to use these in a more casual situation with other annuals or biennials, so a larger space is suitable for the seedlings. Thelesperma self-sows extremely dependably.

Spiderwort, Virginia Day Flower
Forgiving

43. **Latin Name** *Tradescantia* spp.
    tra-dess-CAN-tee-uh species
    Common Name SPIDERWORT, VIRGINIA DAY FLOWER
    Height 2 feet
    Spacing 1 foot on center
    Bloom Time April to frost
    Range All over the United States
    Perennial
    Sun, Part Sun, Dappled Shade, Shade
    Propagation Seed sown in the fall, division of clumps
    Germination 30 days at 70° F

Tradescantia will live in almost any situation. Its 1-inch flowers bloom every morning and close when the sun gets hot. The straight, grass-like leaves provide a pleasing variation of texture among other flowers. I use *Tradescantia* as an accent in my garden and weed out any seedlings. It would also be appropriate massed under a tree, where you would want it to seed out and get really thick. I have not labeled this *Tradescantia* more specifically because it is a hybrid. Carroll Abbott of Greenhills planted several species to get seed. They had indiscriminate sex, so he sold the seed as *T. conglomerata*. The plant shown is an offspring. *Tradescantia* comes in a range of colors—purple, blue, pink, white, and white with a lavender throat. Purple-blue is the most common color.

42. Greenthread
Thelesperma filifolium
Heard Natural Science Museum

43. Spiderwort
Tradescantia spp.
Sally Wasowski

44. **Latin Name**   *Verbena bipinnatifida*
      ver-BEAN-uh bye-pin-nay-TIFF-uh-duh

**Prairie
Verbena
*Picky, Picky,
Picky***

Common Name   PRAIRIE VERBENA
Height   Up to 1 foot, sprawling
Spacing   1 foot on center
Bloom Time   April to frost
Range   South Dakota to Mexico, Alabama to Colorado
Perennial
Sun
Propagation   Seed, fall cuttings, division of clumps
      Germination 20–25 days at 70–75° F, darkness needed

You'd think that a plant that could adjust to so many soils and temperatures would grow anywhere. But I have a lot of trouble with it. I've begun to wonder if it really *is* a perennial. Every single year I fail to get one to winter-over. In the spring, self-sown seed germinates, and by April new plants are blooming. Aside from the fact that I can never keep one alive for more than one year at a time, the only other trouble I've had with this verbena is that I have more than once killed it with shade and water (conditions which its cousin, *V. elegans*, loves). With sun and neglect it is wonderful, needing just an occasional watering to keep it green and blooming all summer. *V. bipinnatifida* is naturally hybridizing with *V. canadensis*, a spring-blooming variety sold in the eastern part of the United States and found over most of Texas.

---

45. **Latin Name**   *Verbena elegans* var. *asperata*
      ver-BEAN-uh el-ee-GANZ variety as-per-A-tuh

**Hardy
Verbena
*Extremely
Useful***

Common Name   HARDY VERBENA
Height   Up to 1 foot
Spacing   1 foot on center
Bloom Time   April to frost
Range   Duval and Hidalgo counties in Texas, Mexico
Perennial, Evergreen
Sun to Dappled Shade
Propagation   Cuttings, division of clumps, seed
      Germination 20–25 days at 70–75° F, darkness needed

V. elegans is already widely sold in our nurseries. It is ever-blooming as long as the temperatures stay above freezing, and evergreen above 15° F. When temperatures drop below 15° F, it dies. It will tolerate a fair amount of drought but looks better with regular watering. I use this verbena often to cover large spaces or for the edges of beds, because it provides a dependable carpet of color the whole blooming season. Moss verbena (*V. tenuisecta*) is a purple verbena that grows in pockets from North Carolina to California. It reportedly makes an excellent groundcover, losing its leaves below freezing but winter-hardy as far north as Illinois. There are other verbenas on the market. Buy any perennial one you can find.

44. Prairie Verbena
Verbena bipinnatifida
Andy Wasowski

45. Hardy Verbena
Verbena elegans var. *asperata*
Sally Wasowski

46. Ironweed
Vernonia baldwinii
Julie Ryan

47. Pale Leaf Yucca
Yucca pallida
Andy Wasowski

46. **Latin Name**   *Vernonia baldwinii*
     ver-NONE-ee-uh bald-WIN-ee-eye
    Common Name   IRONWEED
    Height   2 feet (up to 5 feet in shade)
    Spacing   1 foot on center
    Bloom Time   August to October
    Range   Edwards Plateau to Minnesota
    Perennial
    Sun to Dappled Shade
    Propagation   Cuttings in early summer, root division in late autumn, fall-sown seed

Ironweed
Blooms When
Most Don't

The chief advantage to ironweed is that it gives you color during our hottest, driest time of the year. With a little watering it will sometimes extend its bloom time, both earlier and later. The clumps get bigger each year, increasing the mass of flowers. The plant is not particularly attractive when not in bloom, because the leaves are coarse and prone to mildew. Texas has several varieties of vernonia, which tend to interbreed. The prettiest one I've ever seen came from a limestone outcrop at Greenhills in Duncanville, Texas. This ironweed is 1½ feet tall with a large, pale pink, very fluffy head of flowers, about 4–5 inches across.

47. **Latin Name**   *Yucca pallida*
     YUCK-uh PAL-uh-duh
    Common Name   PALE LEAF YUCCA
    Height   3–5 feet flower stalk, 1 foot leaves
    Spacing   2 feet on center
    Bloom Time   April, May (10 days)
    Range   South Central Texas to Oklahoma and Arkansas
    Perennial, Evergreen
    Sun to Dappled Shade
    Propagation   Root cuttings

Pale Leaf
Yucca
A New Yucca
to Consider

This version is smaller than most yuccas. The leaves are broad and a soft sage green. It has beautiful white waxy blooms, each 1–2 inches long. The leaves obviously go well in a rock garden or desert setting, but they also combine well with soft, lush plantings. Mass several together in a background or use one or two as an accent. If you want to burglar-proof a window, an effective way is to plant this yucca below the sill. Watering will keep the leaves looking up to garden standards during a hot, dry spell, but drought will not kill an established plant. If it starts looking brown and messy, cut the whole plant back to the ground and it will come back green and strong. Another attractive yucca is the little *Y. arkansana*. Its leaves are very thin and so soft and flexible that sometimes they bend over, making it the yucca I would use in a yard with children or by a pool.

48. Thompson Yucca
Yucca thompsoniana
Benny J. Simpson

49. Zexmenia
Zexmenia hispida
Edith Bettinger

48. **Latin Name** *Yucca thompsoniana*
    YUCK-uh tomp-sone-ee-ANE-uh
    Common Name THOMPSON YUCCA
    Height 6–10 feet
    Spacing 4 feet × 2 feet needed
    Bloom Time April, May
    Range Trans-Pecos and northern Mexico
    Perennial, Evergreen
    Sun to Part Sun
    Propagation Stem or root cuttings

Thompson
Yucca
*A Tree
Yucca*

This is a multi-headed yucca widely used in landscaping for its compact size and general tidiness. Many yuccas get very unkempt, with shaggy brown leaves hanging down; Thompson yucca usually stays better-looking than that. In a cactus garden, its silhouette makes a good contrasting shape to combine with the shrubby yuccas and hesperaloe. This is the best winter-hardy tree yucca for North Central Texas. Don't overwater it. It will take any soil and reflected heat.

49. **Latin Name** *Zexmenia hispida*
    zex-MEN-ee-uh HISS-pea-duh
    Common Name ZEXMENIA
    Height 8 inches–3 feet
    Spacing 2 feet on center
    Bloom Time June to frost
    Range Edwards Plateau to Mexico
    Perennial
    Sun to Dappled Shade
    Propagation Seed, cutting, layering

Zexmenia
*A Profusion
of Flowers*

Little yellow to orange daisy-like flowers literally cover this plant from July until frost. In June they are usually sparse and more yellow than later when it gets really hot. In its natural habitat, it is a 3-foot shrub. Further north, it creeps along the ground, its woody branches sending down roots and gradually increasing its circumference. The leaves are gray-green and sticky. I would not have thought that this plant would be winter-hardy in Dallas–Fort Worth, but my zexmenia survived being frozen, probably because it goes dormant at first frost and leaves nothing above ground that can get hurt. My plant was three years old before it blossomed extensively. It has not seeded out at all.

50. Death Camas
Zigadenus nuttallii
Dr. Geoffrey Stanfor[d]

Death Camas
Don't
Eat It

50. **Latin Name** *Zigadenus nuttallii*
    zig-uh-DEEN-us nut-TAL-ee-eye
    Common Name DEATH CAMAS
    Height 1–2 feet
    Spacing 8 inches on center
    Bloom Time April, May (1–2 weeks)
    Range San Angelo, Texas, to Tennessee and Kansas
    Perennial Bulb
    Sun to Part Sun
    Propagation Division of clumps or seed

Most of the plants in our yards are poisonous—at least in part—but this one is especially toxic! Ingesting the large, black, papery bulb or the seeds or the leaves, fresh or dried, could be fatal. But if you can keep your appetite under control, this is a lovely bulb to use; the flower heads are 3–5 inches long and very dramatic. Plant it between taller Dutch iris and shorter *Phlox divaricata*, or in back of a bed of pansies or thrift. Plant the bulbs around the first of December, 5–6 inches deep. This bulb likes to be well drained. The leaves will die back after renewing the bulb for another year, as in daffodils. Don't cut the leaves until they start to yellow and lie flat.

Especially Drought-Resistant Plants

Plants for a Perennial Garden

Chrysanthemum leucanthemum   **Ox-Eye Daisy**
Echinocereus triglochidiatus   **Claret Cup Cactus**
Hesperaloe parviflora   **Red Yucca**
Liatris spp.   **Gayfeather**
Machaeranthera tanacetifolia   **Tahoka Daisy**
* *Melampodium cinereum*   **Blackfoot Daisy**
Opuntia imbricata   **Walking Stick Cholla**
Opuntia phaeacantha   **Prickly Pear**
Pavonia lasiopetala   **Pavonia**
* *Ratibida columnaris*   **Mexican Hat**
Salvia farinacea   **Mealy Blue Sage**
Salvia greggii   **Cherry Sage**
Thelesperma filifolium   **Greenthread**
Yucca pallida   **Pale Leaf Yucca**
Yucca thompsoniana   **Thompson Yucca**
Zexmenia hispida   **Zexmenia**

Naturalizing Plants

Callirhoe spp.   **Winecup**
* *Gaillardia pulchella*   **Indian Blanket**
Oenothera missouriensis   **Yellow Evening
   Primrose**
Oenothera speciosa   **Pink Evening Primrose**
Prunus rivularis   **Creek Plum**
Rhus aromatica   **Aromatic Sumac**
Rhus glabra   **Smooth Sumac**
Rhus lanceolata   **Prairie Flame-Leaf Sumac**
Rosa foliolosa   **White Prairie Rose**
Rosa setigera   **Climbing Prairie Rose**

Shrubs and Decorative Trees

Anisacanthus wrightii   **Flame Acanthus**
Berberis swaseyi   **Texas Barberry**
Berberis trifoliolata   **Agarito**
Leucophyllum frutescens   **Cenizo**

Acacia wrightii   **Wright Acacia**
Cercis canadensis var. *texensis* or var.
   mexicana   **Redbud**
Chilopsis linearis   **Desert Willow**
Cotinus obovatus   **American Smoke Tree**
Diospyros texana   **Texas Persimmon**
Ilex decidua   **Possumhaw Holly**
Juniperus ashei   **Ashe Juniper**
Juniperus deppeana   **Alligator Juniper**
Prunus mexicana   **Mexican Plum**
Rhus virens   **Evergreen Sumac**
Sophora affinis   **Eve's Necklace**
Sophora secundiflora   **Texas Mountain Laurel**
Ungnadia speciosa   **Mexican Buckeye**

Shade Trees

Maclura pomifera   **Bois d'Arc**
Prosopis glandulosa   **Honey Mesquite**
Quercus fusiformis   **Escarpment Live Oak**
Quercus glaucoides   **Lacey Oak**
Quercus pungens var. *vaseyana*   **Vasey Oak**
Quercus texana   **Texas Red Oak**

Vines

Campsis radicans   **Trumpet Vine**

*Will not bloom all summer without supplemental watering

DESERT ROCK GARDEN

I couldn't think of anything else to call this plan, but "desert rock garden" is a misnomer on several accounts. North Central Texas is definitely not a desert, and the typical desert growth with wide spaces of bare dirt around each plant is not going to happen unless you want to weed every week. Furthermore, a rock garden is classically a natural-looking pile of rocks that features alpine plants. Though we have the dryness and reflected light, we have far more heat here than many mountain plants are able to withstand. However, if you want to try to achieve the desert garden or rock garden look here, these are some of the plants you need to use. I used stone walls instead of natural-looking rock outcroppings because there is no way one yard of outcroppings is going to look natural in a typical suburban community.

What this plan shows is what you can do in a very tough situation. The lot faces due south, so there is sun all day. There are no trees around. The ground slopes steeply, letting most of the water run off and exposing more surface directly to the sun. The evaporation is intense. Now, let's really make it rough—this is a rental property, and your tenants may not be enthusiastic about watering the yard, yet expect you to keep it looking nice.

This plan features plants that will take this kind of abuse *once they are established*. There is no mowing and very little pruning involved. Once the plants cover the ground, you will have maximum moisture retention and minimal weeding. The side walls are existing retaining walls made of reinforced concrete to allow the driveways to be at a more reasonable slope. The front wall and the steps are of mortared limestone. All of the other walls are of unmortared limestone. Use sandstone if you live in a sandstone area. The walls are necessary to terrace the slope, because water will soak into flat surfaces better, thus making it easier for the plants to establish themselves. The stone walls are also invaluable in that they retain moisture and provide a cool place for the roots to grow.

The main walking areas are mortared. This has many benefits. One is that people in high heels can walk comfortably. Another is that the water drains off into the slope where it is needed. Still another is that the drought-hardy roses and the live oak (*Quercus fusiformis*) cannot sucker or spread where you don't want them to. The patio continues under the live oak but is unmortared, so that

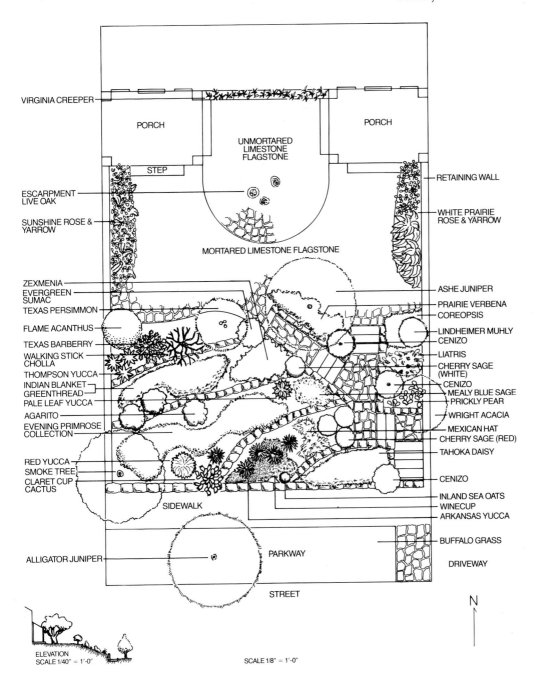

VIRGINIA CREEPER

PORCH

PORCH

UNMORTARED
LIMESTONE
FLAGSTONE

STEP

RETAINING WALL

ESCARPMENT
LIVE OAK

WHITE PRAIRIE
ROSE & YARROW

SUNSHINE ROSE &
YARROW

MORTARED LIMESTONE FLAGSTONE

ZEXMENIA
EVERGREEN
SUMAC
TEXAS PERSIMMON

ASHE JUNIPER

PRAIRIE VERBENA
COREOPSIS

FLAME ACANTHUS

LINDHEIMER MUHLY
CENIZO

TEXAS BARBERRY

LIATRIS

WALKING STICK
CHOLLA

CHERRY SAGE
(WHITE)

THOMPSON YUCCA

CENIZO

INDIAN BLANKET
GREENTHREAD

MEALY BLUE SAGE
PRICKLY PEAR

PALE LEAF YUCCA

WRIGHT ACACIA

AGARITO

MEXICAN HAT

EVENING PRIMROSE
COLLECTION

CHERRY SAGE (RED)

TAHOKA DAISY

RED YUCCA
SMOKE TREE
CLARET CUP
CACTUS

CENIZO

INLAND SEA OATS
WINECUP
ARKANSAS YUCCA

SIDEWALK

BUFFALO GRASS

ALLIGATOR JUNIPER

PARKWAY

DRIVEWAY

STREET

N

ELEVATION
SCALE 1/40" = 1'-0"

SCALE 1/8" = 1'-0"

Desert Rock Garden

the Virginia creeper and tree can benefit from rain water, and not too much water washes down the slope.

The stones and evergreens and the trunk of the persimmon (*Diospyros texana*) assure beauty in the winter. The small trees give interest and ultimately some relief from the sun. The grasses are carefully placed so their seeds will not fall in the garden. The flowers cover the ground and spread or seed themselves out, getting more profuse each year. You should have lots of green rosettes every winter. After a very dry fall, take the time to water some to help seeds to germinate.

The buffalo grass will form a hardy groundcover which needs no mowing. Plant the seed as thickly as you can afford. It will save you time and money later because you will have to do less weeding until it is so thickly established that it keeps the weeds out on its own.

Low-maintenance garden with gaillardia, pink evening primrose, and cherry tree.

Sally Wasowski

Naturalizing Plants

A NATURALIZING PLANT is one that grows in a natural-looking manner, without appearing cultivated or landscaped. My first instinct was to ignore this category of plants; because they sucker (send out subterranean roots that pop up new plants where you least expect them) I felt that, if you used them, you might grow to hate them—and me.

But I had second thoughts. Some are very attractive, like the rose. Others have different characteristics to recommend them; the dogwood thrives in shady places, the elderberry does very well in poorly drained areas, and the sumac is lovely in the fall. Some of the flowers in this section can be used in a more cultivated flower garden, but be prepared to spend some time digging deep to restrain the roots and to prevent these plants from overtaking more timid types. These are the aggressive ones.

Winecup
*Vivid
Wine Red*

51. **Latin Name** *Callirhoe involucrata*
 kah-leer-O-ee in-vo-loo-CRAY-tuh
 Common Name WINECUP
 Height 6 inches to 1 foot
 Spacing 2 feet on center
 Bloom Time May to June
 Range Texas north to Canada
 Perennial Tuber
 Sun
 Propagation Seed in fall or tubers in fall or winter

Winecups like sun and a well-drained bed. These plants send out weak trailing stems from a central tuber. They are green all year except in late summer, when they disappear for one to two months. They do best naturalized on a sloping lawn. If your yard lacks sunny spots, they'll do fine in a big clay pot placed in any sunny area, where they look very attractive cascading over the sides. I like to intermix them with other flowers; black-eyed susans are a particular favorite. When the black-eyed susans die with first frost, the leaves of the winecup get big and green. As the winecups fade and thin, the black-eyed susans that reseeded themselves take over for the summer without disturbing the winecup tubers. If the winecup is planted alone, you can get it to bloom far into the summer if you give it supplemental watering and cut off the old blossoms. *C. leicocarpa* is an annual winecup which comes in a lovely pale pink as well as white and rose.

**Rough Leaf
Dogwood**
*A Solution
for Shade*

52. **Latin Name** *Cornus drummondii*
 KOR-nus druh-MUN-dee-eye
 Common Name ROUGH LEAF DOGWOOD
 Height 15 feet
 Spacing 5–10 feet on center
 Bloom Time April, May (1 week)
 Range Central and East Texas to Virginia and Ontario
 Perennial
 Part Sun to Shade
 Propagation Seed when ripe, cuttings

This small tree or shrub bears little resemblance to the flowering dogwood (*C. florida*), whose white bracts make the "flower" we all know. Rough leaf dogwood actually has a white flower cluster 3 inches wide, but it is not very conspicuous, because the flowers appear after the leaves have come out and only last a week. In late summer the fruits are white and ripe, but the birds like them so much that you rarely get to see them. The leaves are soft and furry instead of shiny, unattractively limp in the summer, but turn a lovely orange-red in the fall. The chief advantage of this plant is that it will form a thicket under those big shady trees where nothing else will grow. Though naturally shrubby, it can be pruned to a tree shape for a lighter, more graceful, appearance.

51. Winecup
Callirhoe spp.
Dr. Geoffrey Stanford

52. Rough Leaf Dogwood
Cornus drummondii
Sally Wasowski

53. **Latin Name** *Engelmannia pinnatifida*
eng-gel-MAN-ee-uh pin-nay-TEE-fee-duh

Cut-Leaf Daisy, Engelmann Daisy *Takes a Siesta*

Common Name CUT-LEAF DAISY, ENGELMANN DAISY
Height 2 feet, rarely 3 feet
Spacing 1 foot on center
Bloom Time April, May, and sparsely thereafter if watered
Range Kansas, Louisiana, Texas, Arizona
Perennial
Sun or Part Sun
Propagation Fall-sown seed or division of clumps

Engelmannia is very showy when in bloom, with the 1-inch blossoms scattered all over the plant. This is not a good cut flower or patio flower because the blooms close up in late afternoon. The name "cut-leaf" comes from the deeply divided leaf, which is big and bristly. If you can water it enough all summer, you can keep the leaves green until the new rosettes come out in the fall. Otherwise, it is dormant in the summer. I prefer this flower in the middle of a bed, where it has lots of room to flop and spread. It is a relative of the Mexican natives *Zinnia*, *Cosmos*, and *Dahlia*. *Engelmannia* has a long stout taproot and transplants any time, but best in winter, when it is in its rosette state.

---

54. **Latin Name** *Eryngium leavenworthii*
ee-RING-ee-um le-ven-WORTH-ee-eye

Eryngo *Not What You Think*

Common Name ERYNGO (ee-RING-o)
Height 2–3 feet
Spacing 1 foot on center
Bloom Time August, September
Range Kansas to Texas
Annual
Sun, Part Sun
Propagation Seed sown in fall or spring
Germination 5–10 days at 65–75° F

Most people think eryngo is a thistle. It isn't, although it is easy to see why there is some confusion. It has prickly leaves and a fuzzy flower, and at all stages of its growth it is extremely sharp and full of stickers. This is why it is in the naturalizing section instead of with the high-class stuff. I would even go so far as to urge you to wear gloves when weeding around it and, of course, when you pull out the dead plants after first frost. Naturally, I do not recommend planting near a walkway. Although this flower tends to photograph hot pink, it is in reality a deep purple blue with brilliant blue stamens. Each head is 2 to 3 inches long. It makes a good cut flower and keeps its shape when dried, but loses its wonderful color. Some people spray them with paint, and others just use them for their distinctive shape in dried flower arrangements. The seed is best planted as soon as it ripens in the fall.

53. Cut-Leaf Daisy
Engelmannia pinnatifida
Sally Wasowski

54. Eryngo
Eryngium leavenworthii
Edith Bettinger

Indian Blanket, Firewheel
No Need to Fertilize

55. **Latin Name** *Gaillardia pulchella*
gay-LARD-ee-uh pull-KELL-uh
Common Name INDIAN BLANKET, FIREWHEEL
Height 1–2 feet
Spacing 1 foot on center
Bloom Time May to frost if watered
Range Texas and Louisiana to Missouri
Annual
Sun to Part Sun
Propagation Fall-sown seed
Germination 15–20 days at 70° F

If your gaillardias are crowded enough, if the soil is poor enough, if there is some shade, and they have genes that think small, this flower can be an absolute delight all summer and autumn until frost. Otherwise, you might have to cut it down in mid-summer because it is so aggressive. Water it a little or it will die in June like those in the fields. As a cut flower it lasts a long time. Let it go to seed about August so it will be overcrowded again next year. Transplant or weed out all seedlings that are not exactly where you want them. Occasionally gaillardia sports variations in color such as cream and yellow, peach, coral, peach with yellow tips, red with white tips, and all red. There are obvious possibilities for breeding here. Breeding has been done with *Gaillardia X grandiflora* neat mounded plants, but their longevity and usefulness in Texas summers has not been proven.

Maximilian Daisy
Photosensitive

56. **Latin Name** *Helianthus maximiliani*
heel-ee-AN-thus max-ee-mill-ee-ANE-ee
Common Name MAXIMILIAN DAISY
Height 2–3 feet or more
Spacing 1 foot on center
Bloom Time August, September, October
Range Central Texas to Canada
Perennial
Sun to Part Sun
Propagation Seed or division of roots

Don't plant Maximilian daisy under an outside light! It might not think the days are short enough for it to bloom before frost comes and it dies back. It likes good soil and requires extra water during its blooming period, in the hottest part of the summer. Each plant is tall and thin at first, but after a few years of rooting out underground, it is a huge clump. It looks most effective massed at the back of the garden. Because the 2-to3-inch flowers leave the bottom halves of the stalks bare, it is important to position shorter plants in front. *Eupatorium* would be my personal choice; its lavender blue is a stunning contrast to the sunflower's brilliant yellow. They bloom about the same time and have similar soil and water requirements.

55. Indian Blanket
Gaillardia pulchella
Andy Wasowski

56. Maximilian Daisy
Helianthus maximiliani
Julie Ryan

93

57. Texas Bluebonnet
Lupinus texensis
Julie Ryan

Texas
Bluebonnet
One of the
Five State
Flowers of
Texas

57. **Latin Name** *Lupinus texensis*
lou-PINE-us tex-EN-sis
Common Name TEXAS BLUEBONNET
Height 1½ feet
Spacing 1½ feet on center
Bloom Time April
Range Central Texas
Annual
Sun

There are five species of bluebonnets, each indigenous to at least one part of Texas; they are *all* the state flower. This means that all Texans, no matter where in the state they live, can grow an official state flower in their own yards.

L. texensis is the most widespread, growing through North Central Texas down to San Antonio and from Brenham to San Angelo.

L. subcarnosus is found all through the sandy soils of East Central Texas.

L. havardii, huge and deep blue, is found in the Big Bend.

L. concinnus, not as showy, grows in the Franklin Mountains near El Paso, into Mexico and New Mexico.

L. plattensis is found in the sand dunes of the Texas Panhandle and more prolifically in states north and west of there.

Bluebonnets are easy to plant from seed, but the seed coat is very hard. This keeps the seed viable for a great number of years, surviving the worst that nature can dish out. Eventually, general wear-and-tear penetrates the seed coat and germination begins in the fall rains. To speed up this process, you could use a file to break the seed coat, but you can imagine how time-consuming this would be! An easier way is to buy treated seed. This seed is combined with sand in a cement mixer— the gritty sand scarifying or scratching the seed coat. If the seed has been treated, it will say so on the package. Green Horizons in Kerrville, Texas, is a good source.

Many people advise soaking the seed overnight, but this has been proven to be unnecessary, and more than one night's soaking can lower the germination rate. It is best to plant the seed in September while the soil is still warm, as a soil temperature of 55–70° F is essential for germination, which takes up to twenty days. It's easiest of all to buy a plant in September or October and plant it just where you want it. It will grow roots all winter, gradually enlarging its rosette. In spring, the top growth will be rapid; by mid-April or sooner, your plant will be in its month of glory.

Watch a bee pollinate a flower. The bee lands on the keel. The weight of its body opens the wings of the flower so the bee can drink the nectar and wade through the pollen. After a flower is pollinated and the nectar is gone, the bluebonnet considerately turns its little white spot to red so another bee won't waste time and be disappointed investigating that flower again.

If you think bluebonnets are a lot of work for a month of pleasure, take comfort by remembering that the bluebonnet, being a legume, will add nitrogen to your soil, if you leave it until the top turns brown. To have bluebonnets next year, you will need to buy new plants or sow seed all over again. You can gather your own seed just as the pods start turning gray and before they split. When they split, they shoot the seed up to fifty feet away. So don't think they will seed out in place and provide you with a lifetime of bluebonnets—unless, of course, you have planted a whole meadow. It often takes two to three years of planting seed in the same place for them to take hold.

Another note of caution: Don't buy a plant in the spring and expect to get a 1½-foot mound of bluebonnets. You will probably get just the one bloom you brought home from the nursery.

Bergamont,
Beebalm
Mint Family

58.　**Latin Name**　*Monarda fistulosa*
　　　mo-NARD-uh FIST-u-low-suh
Common Name　BERGAMONT, BEEBALM
Height　2 feet
Spacing　1 foot on center
Bloom Time　June to September
Range　Maine to Minnesota, Florida to Texas
Perennial
Sun to Dappled Shade
Propagation　Seed anytime, summer cuttings, division of clumps
　　　Germination 15–20 days at 60–70° F

You can always tell mint, because the stems are square instead of round and the leaves have a pleasantly pungent fragrance when crushed. *Monarda* attracts butterflies and hummingbirds. This plant is almost too easy to grow. It spreads very rapidly and is difficult to control. It will bloom in the shade, but is susceptible to mildew there. It will wilt if the ground is dry enough to crack, but I've never managed to kill any off. It is a good plant to use when you want a big bed of summer color. After the plant dies down at frost, cut off the brown; in early spring new growth will appear. *M. didyma*, native to the northeastern United States, comes in red, does well here, and has a root system much easier to control. *M. citriodora*, the annual, blooms from May to October if you keep it watered, but I've usually found that it mildews. I suspect it does better further west where the air is drier.

Ozark
Sun Drop,
Fluttermill,
Yellow
Evening
Primrose
*Blooms
All Night*

59.　**Latin Name**　*Oenothera missouriensis*
　　　ee-no-THEE-ruh muh-zoo-ree-EN-sis
Common Name　OZARK SUN DROP, FLUTTERMILL, YELLOW EVENING
　　　PRIMROSE
Height　1 foot
Spacing　1 foot on center
Bloom Time　April to July
Range　Missouri, Nebraska, south to North Central Texas and the
　　　Edwards Plateau
Perennial
Sun to Part Sun
Propagation　Seed or division of crown

This evening primrose will grow out of limestone outcroppings and take extreme drought. It tends to sprawl, holding its 3–5-inch flowers face upward. Sometimes the flowers have no stems, other times they look just like the photo. The blossoms open in late afternoon and close when the sun gets hot the following morning. After it sets seed, the plant goes dormant. So I recommend planting it near a lantana or pavonia, because they greatly expand their growth each summer, covering the bare spot left by the oenothera. Then they get cut back each winter, allowing room for the oenothera's return in the spring. The visually

58. Bergamont
Monarda fistulosa
Benny J. Simpson

59. Yellow Evening Primrose
Oenothera missouriensis
Benny J. Simpson

59. Diamond Petal Evening Primrose
Oenothera rhombipetala
Edith Bettinger

similar *O. rhombipetala* (four-point or diamond petal evening primrose) blooms all summer—a distinct advantage. This biennial grows in 2–3-foot mounds on sandy and clay soils. The mound is sufficiently airy to permit the one-year plants to develop under it, so you can keep one spot in your garden for this primrose year after year. It is especially lovely when the sun catches the translucent petals.

60. Pink Evening Primrose
Oenothera speciosa
Dr. Geoffrey Stanford

61. Creek Plum
Prunus rivularis
Dr. Geoffrey Stanford

61. Creek Plum
Prunus rivularis
Benny J. Simpson

60. **Latin Name**   *Oenothera speciosa*
    ee-no-THEE-ruh spee-see-OH-suh
    Common Name   PINK EVENING PRIMROSE
    Height   1 foot
    Spacing   Start with one
    Bloom Time   April to June
    Range   Texas to Illinois, South Carolina, Arizona, and Mexico
    Perennial
    Sun to Part Sun
    Propagation   Seed or division of roots

Pink Evening
Primrose
Open 9 to 5

Why does an evening primrose open in the daytime? *O. speciosa* is actually *two* species of primrose—one opening in the morning and one at night. But there's been so much hanky-panky between them, resulting in a muddled gene pool, that you might as well consider them as one. If you have a well-ordered and well-weeded garden, *do not* put this plant in it. If you have a garden that is supposed to take care of itself, you will probably get a lot of enjoyment from this plant. It does best in a grassy parkway where it is contained by concrete and can be mowed after blooming. It can also grow in a clay pot, looking magnificent on your patio all spring. But, once the blooms are gone, you're left with thin, unattractive foliage—so hide the pot behind the garage until next year.

61. **Latin Name**   *Prunus rivularis*
    PROO-nus rih-view-LAIR-is
    Common Name   HOG PLUM, CREEK PLUM
    Height   To 6 feet
    Spacing   4–5 feet on center
    Bloom Time   March, April
    Range   Edwards Plateau north to Oklahoma
    Perennial
    Sun to Part Sun
    Propagation   Seed sown the depth of the plum as soon as ripe

Hog Plum,
Creek Plum
*White Thicket
in Early
Spring*

Little suckering plums are useful for an understory in a wooded area, or at the end of a long back yard. One reason to have them is that they make a beautiful cloud of white blossoms in the spring. Another is that their plums are a sure way to attract birds. Because they make new plants by sending out roots, do not put these in a situation you want to control. *P. rivularis* is the healthiest suckering plum for limestone soils. Its plums are yellow with a red blush and ripen in July and August. If you have sand, you might prefer *P. angustifolia*, because of its red and yellow plums, which ripen in early summer. It grows more tree-like, up to 12 feet high.

Aromatic Sumac, Fragrant Sumac, Three-Leaved Sumac
Not Poisonous

62. **Latin Name** *Rhus aromatica*
    RUSS or RUSE err-o-MAT-eh-kuh
Common Name AROMATIC SUMAC, FRAGRANT SUMAC, THREE-LEAVED SUMAC
Height 5–6 feet
Spacing 4 feet on center
Bloom Time Late February
Range Eastern half of the United States
Perennial
Sun to Dappled Shade
Propagation Seed

Though this is a three-leaved sumac, it does not resemble poison ivy or poison sumac (which actually has five to thirteen leaflets). Its leaves are not only touchable, but give off a delicious fragrance when you rub them, giving this sumac the name "aromatic." This delightful little shrub is best used in a naturalizing situation, because it suckers and forms thickets. It is covered with tiny yellow flowers very early in the spring before it gets its leaves. The small berries turn red in April and are greedily gobbled up by the birds. All summer, it is a small neat shrub, with cute leaves and a delicate fragrance. Then, in fall, it turns orange and scarlet, though not as brilliantly as *R. glabra*. *R. aromatica* grows either on limestone or in sand.

Prairie Flame-Leaf Sumac
Red Berries All Winter

63. **Latin Name** *Rhus lanceolata*
    RUSS or RUSE lan-see-o-LAY-tuh
Common Name PRAIRIE FLAME-LEAF SUMAC
Height Up to 30 feet
Spacing 20 feet on center
Bloom Time July, August
Range Central Texas to Oklahoma and Mexico, New Mexico
Perennial
Sun to Dappled Shade
Propagation Seed

This is naturally a very open tree, not requiring pruning. The leaves are a dark, shiny green. The flowers are in panicles 6 inches long, as shown. The fruits ripen in the fall and not only attract birds, notably quail, but are pretty throughout the winter. The tree's big moment of glory is in the fall, when the leaves turn a brilliant scarlet. Smooth sumac (*R. glabra*), with a natural range stretching from Arizona to Quebec, is more shrubby, grows to 12 feet tall, blooms in the late spring, and is even more brilliant in the fall. Both these sumacs grow equally well in limestone soils or sand, and both sucker.

62. Aromatic Sumac
Rhus aromatica
Heard Natural Science Museum

62. Aromatic Sumac
Rhus aromatica
Dr. Geoffrey Stanford

62. Aromatic Sumac
Rhus aromatica
Heard Natural Science Museum

63. Prairie Flame-Leaf Sumac
Rhus lanceolata
Dr. Geoffrey Stanford

63. Smooth Sumac
Rhus glabra
Julie Ryan

63. Prairie Flame-Leaf Sumac
Rhus lanceolata
Julie Ryan

64. White Prairie Rose
Rosa foliolosa
Edith Bettinger

65. Climbing Prairie Rose
Rosa setigera
Benny J. Simpson

102

64. **Latin Name**   *Rosa foliolosa* var. *alba*
     ROSE-uh foe-lee-o-LOW-suh variety ALL-buh
     Common Name   WHITE PRAIRIE ROSE, LEAFY ROSE
     Height   20 inches
     Spacing   3 feet on center
     Bloom Time   May to June (2–3 weeks)
     Range   Prairies in Texas, Arkansas, and Oklahoma
     Perennial
     Sun to Part Sun
     Propagation   Seed, dormant cuttings in January, layering

White
Prairie Rose,
Leafy Rose
*Covers a Lot
of Ground*

Well-contained, or if you don't care where it goes, this rose can be a delight. The flowers are 1½–2 inches wide, satiny, opened wide to show the golden stamens. The leaflets are dark green, shiny, and slender. The stems are not particularly thorny for a rose. The plant is relatively disease-free and very long-lived. It doesn't branch densely, but stems pop up everywhere, although not thickly. It looks best when inter-planted with other low-growing flowers such as *Achillea* or *Thelesperma*. Sometimes this rose has a pink blossom. A low-growing rose that is usu-ally pink is the sunshine rose (*R. suffulta*). It is exceedingly thorny and bristly. It grows from North Central Texas to Canada, and blooms from May to August. Its blossom looks much like the picture, but it is deli-cately suffused with pink.

---

65. **Latin Name**   *Rosa setigera*
     ROSE-uh seh-TIJ-er-uh
     Common Name   CLIMBING PRAIRIE ROSE
     Height   Climbing rose
     Spacing   6 feet on center
     Bloom Time   May to June
     Range   Eastern half of the United States
     Perennial
     Sun or Part Sun
     Propagation   Seed, layering, dormant cuttings in January

Climbing
Prairie Rose
Disease-Free

The lovely 2-inch roses bloom at the ends of canes which grow 6–15 feet long. Not at all delicate, this rose suckers and climbs vigorously. Once a rose has started to sucker, it is extremely hard to dig up and transplant. In fact, once you have this rose, like it or not, you will prob-ably have it forever. Obviously not for your rose garden, this plant's main advantage is its health. If you could contain the roots in a space within a concrete patio, for instance, the tops could be easily restrained by pruning. Always prune only after it blooms. This rose is bare-branched in the winter. The rose hips are orange and are good bird food.

66. Elderberry
Sambucus canadensis
Heard Natural Science Mus

66. Elderberry
Sambucus canadensis
Sally Wasowski

66. Elderberry
Sambucus canadensis
Andy Wasowski

Elderberry
Likes
Moist Soils

66. **Latin Name** *Sambucus canadensis*
  sam-BUKE-us kan-uh-DEN-sis
Common Name ELDERBERRY
Height To 12 feet
Spacing 20 feet on center
Bloom Time May, June
Range Eastern half of North America
Perennial
Sun to Part Sun
Propagation Seed, hardwood and softwood cuttings, root
  cuttings

This plant is the one that I would recommend for an understory or thicket by a stream or lake. The flowers are tiny, but arranged in huge clusters up to a foot across, making the plant very noticeable in early summer. The fruits in fall are almost equally conspicuous, the same shape as the big flower heads. They are red, turning black as they mature. The berries are eaten by about forty-five species of birds. Since this plant suckers, I would not recommend its use in a garden. I have seen lone plants on dry land in a yard, so it might not sucker out of the moist bottomlands. I don't know how much water is required to keep the plant healthy in the summer. The seeds do require moisture to germinate, doing best under a faucet or drain spout.

Plants to Attract Birds

Plants for a Perennial Garden

Asclepius tuberosa **Butterfly Weed**
Lobelia cardinalis **Cardinal Flower**
Penstemon murrayanus **Scarlet Penstemon**
Salvia coccinea **Scarlet Sage**
Salvia greggii **Cherry Sage**

Shrubs and Decorative Trees

Anisacanthus wrightii **Flame Acanthus**
Chilopsis linearis **Desert Willow**

Vines

Bignonia capreolata **Crossvine**
Campsis radicans **Trumpet Vine**
Gelsemium sempervirens **Carolina Jessamine**
Ipomoea quamoclit **Cypress Vine**
Lonicera sempervirens **Coral Honeysuckle**

OTHER BIRDS

Plants for a Perennial Garden

Aquilegia (all kinds) **Columbine**
Chrysanthemum leucanthemum **Ox-Eye Daisy**
Coreopsis (all kinds) **Golden Wave**
Echinacea (all kinds) **Coneflower**
Malvaviscus drummondii **Turk's Cap**
Rudbeckia (all kinds) **Black-Eyed Susan, etc.**

Naturalizing Plants

Cornus drummondii **Rough Leaf Dogwood**
Helianthus maximiliani **Maximilian Daisy**
Prunus rivularis **Creek Plum**
Rhus (all kinds) **Sumac**
Rosa (all kinds) **Rose**
Sambucus canadensis **Elderberry**

Shrubs and Decorative Trees

Berberis swaseyi **Texas Barberry**
Berberis trifoliolata **Agarito**
Callicarpa americana **American Beauty Berry**
Lonicera albiflora **Honeysuckle Bush**
Arbutus xalapensis **Texas Madrone**
Cephalanthus occidentalis **Button Bush**

Chilopsis linearis **Desert Willow**
Crataegus reverchonii **Hawthorn**
Diospyros texana **Texas Persimmon**
Ilex decidua **Possumhaw Holly**
Ilex vomitoria **Yaupon Holly**
Juniperus ashei **Ashe Juniper**
Juniperus deppeana **Alligator Juniper**
Myrica cerifera **Wax Myrtle**
Prunus mexicana **Mexican Plum**
Rhamnus caroliniana **Carolina Buckthorn**
Rhus virens **Evergreen Sumac**
Viburnum rufidulum **Rusty Blackhaw Viburnum**

Shade Trees

Fraxinus texensis **Texas Ash**
Liquidamber styraciflua **Sweetgum**
Magnolia grandiflora **Southern Magnolia**
Sapindus saponaria **Soapberry**
Taxodium distichum **Bald Cypress**
Ulmus americana **American Elm**

Vines

Parthenocissus quinquefolia **Virginia Creeper**

Plants for Poor Drainage

Plants for a Perennial Garden

Cooperia drummondii   **Rain Lily**
Eupatorium coelestinum   **Blue Boneset**
Habranthus texanus   **Copper Lily**
Hibiscus coccineus   **Texas Star Hibiscus**
Hymenocallis liriosme   **Spider Lily**
Iris brevicaulis   **Louisiana Iris**
Lantana horrida   **Texas Lantana**
Physostegia pulchella   **Lionheart** (Spring)

Naturalizing Plants

Sambucus canadensis   **Elderberry**

Shrubs and Decorative Trees

Aesculus pavia   **Scarlet Buckeye**
Amorpha fruticosa   **False Indigo**

Cephalanthus occidentalis   **Button Bush**
Crataegus reverchonii   **Hawthorn**
Myrica cerifera   **Wax Myrtle**
Sophora affinis   **Eve's Necklace**

Shade Trees

Catalpa bignonioides   **Catalpa**
Liquidamber styraciflua   **Sweetgum**
Magnolia grandiflora   **Southern Magnolia**
Taxodium distichum   **Bald Cypress**
Ulmus crassifolia   **Cedar Elm**

Vines

Bignonia capreolata   **Crossvine**
Clematis pitcheri   **Leatherflower**
Passiflora incarnata   **Passion Flower**

Plants for Fall Berries

Naturalizing Plants

Rhus glabra   **Smooth Sumac**
Rhus lanceolata   **Prairie Flame-Leaf Sumac**
Rosa foliolosa   **White Prairie Rose**
Rosa setigera   **Climbing Prairie Rose**

Shrubs and Decorative Trees

Callicarpa americana   **American Beauty Bush**
Lonicera albiflora   **Honeysuckle Bush**

Crataegus reverchonii   **Hawthorn**
Ilex decidua   **Possumhaw Holly**
Ilex vomitoria   **Yaupon Holly**

Vines

Clematis pitcheri (fluffy seeds)   **Leatherflower**

BIRD GARDEN

This is a very easy-going garden; it allows you to devote as much or as little time to upkeep as you wish. And it has the essentials for the serious birdwatcher. There is a creek to provide a place for the birds to drink and bathe, and for water-loving plants such as elderberry (*Sambucus canadensis*) and button bush (*Cephalanthus occidentalis*). You may even find your garden is attracting fowl normally found around local lakes and ponds, so you'll have a greater variety to observe.

The house is on a steep slope above the creek. Retaining walls divide the slope into three levels for easy planting and access from house to creek. The flagstone terraces provide two vantages from which to bird-watch. The gardens around the house are fairly dry and are landscaped with drought-resistant plants in a rather formal manner. Each level gets progressively moister and wilder, gradually employing more of the suckering plants to make thickets.

Birds not only like a wide range of seeds and fruits, but they also require nesting sites. The thickets and trees provide a variety of sites. The magnolia and live oak (*Quercus virginiana*) are especially important nesting places for the winter months. The spaces under the trees can be in lawn or in groundcovers. Both Virginia creeper (*Parthenocissus quinquefolia*) for shade and trumpet vine (*Campsis radicans*) for sunny places make interesting groundcovers which attract birds. The magnolia will take years to reach the size drawn on the plan, so the trumpet vine could be a very showy choice to cover the ground in the meantime. So could the coral honeysuckle (*Lonicera sempervirens*). You might be surprised to see the name "sugarberry" on one of the big shade trees. This is a very close relative of the hackberry, but is a little less warty. I think hackberries are ugly, with those warts all over the leaves and the corky growths on the bark that make climbing them painful. Every yard has an existing hackberry (at least in the seedling stage) and many have existing sugarberries. The reason they are so plentiful is that the birds love the seeds, which are a staple for many of them in the winter. After a freeze, the sugar in the seeds

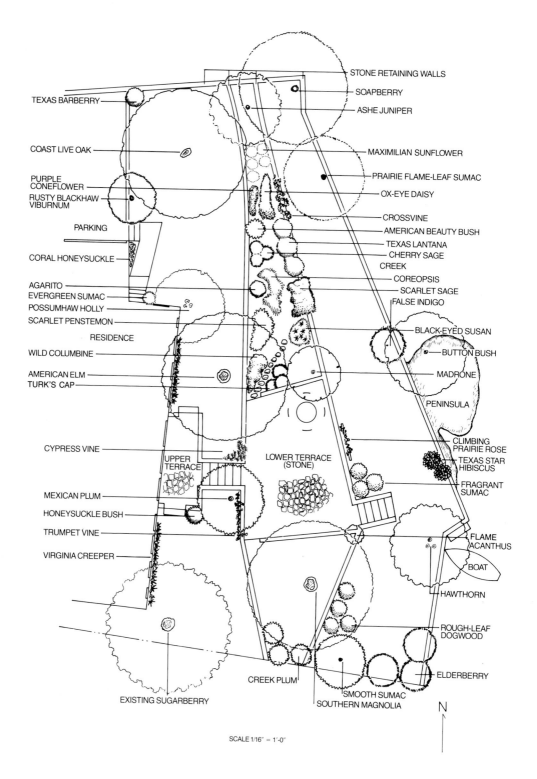

STONE RETAINING WALLS
SOAPBERRY
ASHE JUNIPER
TEXAS BARBERRY
MAXIMILIAN SUNFLOWER
COAST LIVE OAK
PRAIRIE FLAME-LEAF SUMAC
OX-EYE DAISY
PURPLE CONEFLOWER
RUSTY BLACKHAW VIBURNUM
CROSSVINE
AMERICAN BEAUTY BUSH
PARKING
TEXAS LANTANA
CHERRY SAGE
CORAL HONEYSUCKLE
CREEK
COREOPSIS
AGARITO
SCARLET SAGE
EVERGREEN SUMAC
FALSE INDIGO
POSSUMHAW HOLLY
SCARLET PENSTEMON
BLACK-EYED SUSAN
RESIDENCE
BUTTON BUSH
WILD COLUMBINE
MADRONE
AMERICAN ELM
TURK'S CAP
PENINSULA
CYPRESS VINE
CLIMBING PRAIRIE ROSE
UPPER TERRACE
LOWER TERRACE (STONE)
TEXAS STAR HIBISCUS
FRAGRANT SUMAC
MEXICAN PLUM
HONEYSUCKLE BUSH
FLAME ACANTHUS
TRUMPET VINE
BOAT
VIRGINIA CREEPER
HAWTHORN
ROUGH-LEAF DOGWOOD
ELDERBERRY
CREEK PLUM
EXISTING SUGARBERRY
SMOOTH SUMAC
SOUTHERN MAGNOLIA
N

SCALE 1/16" = 1'-0"

Bird Garden

turns to alcohol, producing many drunk birds. I included this tree in the plan because it is such an important source of food for birds.

The purpose of the flower garden is to provide nectar for the hummingbirds and to produce seeds for other birds. Don't cut off the seed heads! Root out ugly weeds and Johnson grass, but otherwise let it get wild and overgrown if you wish. It should be very colorful from spring to frost.

Shady perennial garden with oxalis, veronica, spiderwort, Mexican hat, lantana, gloriosa daisy, day lily (not native), and crape myrtle (not native).

Shrubs and Decorative Trees

THIS SECTION deals with small trees or shrubs. Sometimes these trees send up lots of trunks, or branch low to the ground, and are so short that they more resemble shrubs. If you prune out these lower branches, they make beautiful trees. Some do best as shrubs. I have listed those separately at the beginning.

These decorative trees can have one trunk or be multi-trunked; the tree will be shorter if it is multi-trunked. Branches should be left only on the upper one-third of the tree if you want to grow flowers underneath or see a view. Leave branches on the upper two-thirds if you want to use the tree more as a screen.

Pruning should also be done to clean out the branches that grow inward; cut close to the trunk and leave only those branches that grow upward and outward, and never trim their ends. If you already know how to prune your yaupon holly or your crape myrtle, you can prune any of these small trees. I use these trees as shade trees in small yards, as accents in large yards or perennial gardens, and as understory in a large, wooded situation.

BEST USED AS SHRUBS

Texas Firecracker Plant, Flame Acanthus
Summer Nectar

67. **Latin Name**   *Anisacanthus wrightii*
ah-neese-uh-KAN-thus RIGHT-ee-eye
Common Name   TEXAS FIRECRACKER PLANT, FLAME ACANTHUS
Height   3 feet
Spacing   2 feet on center
Bloom Time   June to frost
Range   Edwards Plateau, northern Mexico
Perennial
Sun to Part Sun
Propagation   Seed (as soon as ripe in the fall) and softwood cuttings, hardwood cuttings in the winter

This small shrub is usually found by small streams in the wild, but it does perfectly well in a barely watered yard or in a patio pot 12 inches or larger. It is delicately covered with small red-tubed flowers all summer and is a great favorite with the hummingbirds and butterflies. It can be pruned to be a low dense shrub or allowed to branch sparingly and gracefully. Though it is not evergreen, the pretty exfoliating bark makes it attractive in the winter. It froze back only a little in Dallas in the Big Freeze; the roots were perfectly hardy. It appears to have no disease or insect problems.

Texas Barberry
Pastel Reds & Purples All Winter

68. **Latin Name**   *Berberis swaseyi*
BER-ber-is SWA-zee-eye
Common Name   TEXAS BARBERRY
Height   3–5 feet
Spacing   2–3 feet on center
Bloom Time   April
Range   Edwards Plateau
Perennial, Evergreen
Sun to Part Sun
Propagation   Seed, 60 days of cold stratification required

This spiny shrub is useful for its contrasting foliage. During the spring and summer, it is a light yellow-green, as illustrated, although some plants are more light gray-green. The leaves are similar to grape holly in shape, but even more full of stickers, so don't use this plant near a walkway. In the autumn, the leaves turn soft, muted shades of reds and purples, which last all winter. In early spring, the flowers appear, bright golden-yellow and very fragrant. The fruits are small, brown, and plump, if there is enough moisture. This is an especially good shrub to use if you need an evergreen shrub that will grow right out of limestone. It can be allowed to grow to its natural shape or it can be sheared. It will be fuller if grown in full sun.

67. Flame Acanthus
Anisacanthus wrightii
Benny J. Simpson

68. Texas Barberry
Berberis swaseyi
Benny J. Simpson

113

Agarito
Evergreen Shrub

69. **Latin Name** *Berberis trifoliolata*
BER-ber-is try-fole-ee-o-LAY-tuh
Common Name AGARITO (ag-uh-REET-oh)
Height 2–6 feet
Spacing 2–3 feet on center
Bloom Time Late February or March
Range South coastal Texas north to Palo Duro Canyon and west to the Trans-Pecos
Perennial, Evergreen
Sun to Dappled Shade
Propagation Seed, planted in fall, or with cold stratification in summer

Agarito is kin to the mahonias or grape hollies currently in the nursery trade. The name *trifoliolata* means "leaves in threes," and perfectly describes the dark green, spiny leaves, which remain green all winter. In very early spring, there is a scattering of fragrant, small, bright yellow blossoms. Birds love the red fruits, which ripen in May amid sharp, prickly leaves. Agarito is dense if grown in full sun. It can be sheared to make an evergreen hedge. In the shade it gets thin and rangy, but graceful. It has a long taproot, making it drought-resistant but difficult to transplant after it gets to be 1–2 feet tall.

American Beauty Berry, French Mulberry
Purple Berries

70. **Latin Name** *Callicarpa americana*
kal-ee-KAR-puh a-mer-ee-CANE-uh
Common Name AMERICAN BEAUTY BERRY, FRENCH MULBERRY
Height 5–7 feet
Spacing 5 feet on center
Bloom Time Berries September, sometimes until March
Range Eastern half of Texas, Maryland to Cuba
Perennial
Sun to Dappled Shade
Propagation Cuttings, seed (slow), or division of clumps

This is a large, sprawling, rounded shrub with nondescript, pale pink flowers in the spring, and big purple or white berries in the fall. This shrub likes moisture and sand, but will also grow out of limestone on a seep line. Because this plant looks its best only when it has berries, I'd recommend against using more than one or two of them in one spot. You might be tempted to use these lovely berries as centerpiece decorations, but don't! They drop off as soon as the twig is cut. Mockingbirds love them and sometimes eat all the berries. If they aren't eaten, they keep their color and stay on the bush all winter.

69. Agarito
Berberis trifoliolata
Benny J. Simpson

69. Agarito
Berberis trifoliolata
Julie Ryan

70. American Beauty Berry
Callicarpa americana
Dr. Geoffrey Stanford

115

Cenizo, Texas Sage, Purple Sage
Contrasting Foliage

71. **Latin Name** *Leucophyllum frutescens*
loo-koe-FILE-um FRUIT-es-sens
Common Name CENIZO, TEXAS SAGE, PURPLE SAGE
Height 3–8 feet
Spacing 2–3 feet on center
Bloom Time Late July and August
Range Southwestern United States and Mexico
Perennial, Somewhat Evergreen
Sun to Part Sun
Propagation Best from softwood tip cuttings

Benny Simpson, at the Texas Agricultural Experiment Station in Dallas, has done many years of research and development on this shrub. He is currently working on a hybrid to combine the best blooming traits of two species. Nurseries are now carrying a compact cenizo and a taller, undeveloped form. The gray-green leaves get sparse around February, and new leaves appear in March. This plant takes intense and reflected heat and is exceedingly drought-resistant. It is supposed to grow slowly and can get rangy if given too much water. Unfortunately, this little shrub seems to be at its northern limit in Dallas; many are killed when the temperature gets down to 5° F. The pretty violet-flowered "compactum" works well in mass plantings or in patio pots. The taller plant is best used as an accent. It can get tree-like and very graceful, with a silvery, twisted trunk.

Honeysuckle Bush
Keeps in Bounds

72. **Latin Name** *Lonicera albiflora*
lon-ISS-er-uh al-bee-FLOOR-uh
Common Name HONEYSUCKLE BUSH
Height 5–8 feet
Spacing 5 feet on center
Bloom Time March, April (2 weeks)
Range Central Texas and Oklahoma
Perennial, Almost Evergreen
Sun to Shade
Propagation Cuttings or seed

This is a real shrub, capable of making an 8-foot mound, but is usually kept trimmed to 5 feet. It does not behave like the Japanese honeysuckle vine that is taking over the eastern half of Texas; left alone, it stays in place. Birds, however, are very fond of its fruit, so this honeysuckle winds up wherever the birds fly. This is an old-fashioned plant, once widely used in our gardens and still to be found in yards planted fifty years ago. It is one of our first flowers to bloom in the spring. It grows by throwing out long viny branches which later fill in. When it is in the viny stage, it has been known to entwine itself on a nearby fence or tree. It needs a little afternoon shade or watering to prevent the leaves from scorching in August.

71. Cenizo
Leucophyllum frutescens
Benny J. Simpson

72. Honeysuckle Bush
Lonicera albiflora
Benny J. Simpson

72. Honeysuckle Bush
Lonicera albiflora
Benny J. Simpson

117

73. Evergreen Sumac
Rhus virens
Benny J. Simpson

74. Wright Acacia
Acacia wrightii
Benny J. Simpson

73. **Latin Name** *Rhus virens*
        RUSS or RUSE VIE-rens
    Common Name EVERGREEN SUMAC
    Height 4–12 feet
    Fall Color Evergreen with red fruits
    Range Edwards Plateau and Trans-Pecos to Mexico
    Sun to Part Sun
    Propagation Seed, softwood cuttings

Evergreen
Sumac
*Evergreen
Shrub or
Small Tree?*

Have you ever wanted a small evergreen tree close to your house, but you didn't want it to grow into your eaves? Did you ever want to use a shrub with a softer, more informal look than a sheared hedge, but your pittosporum kept freezing? Evergreen sumac might be the answer. The compound leaves, consisting of 5 to 9 glossy, dark green leaflets, are 2–5 inches long, first emerging a reddish color. A few may again turn reddish, brown, or yellow in the fall; but the overall appearance will remain green, and no leaves will drop until replaced by new leaves in the spring. The white flowers appear off and on in the late summer after rain. In the fall, the berry clusters ripen into frosted-red sticky fruits. *R. virens* is said to be winter-hardy as far north as Oklahoma, but many suffered damage and died because of the Big Freeze that hit Dallas and areas to the north.

BEST USED AS TREES

74. **Latin Name** *Acacia wrightii*
        uh-KAY-shuh RIGHT-ee-eye
    Common Name WRIGHT ACACIA, TREE CATCLAW
    Height 6–9 feet (sometimes 30 feet near Uvalde)
    Bloom Time April, May
    Range Rio Grande Plains, Trans-Pecos, Edwards Plateau, Rolling Plains, southern United States, northern Mexico
    Sun
    Propagation Seed

Wright
Acacia,
Tree Catclaw
*Our Most
Cold-Hardy
Acacia*

The acacia gives a light dappled shade which is ideal for a garden with limited space. You can have some relief from the sun and the nice private feeling that a tree can give, but you have enough light to grow whatever you want under it. This particular acacia is winter-hardy as far north as Dallas–Fort Worth. It likes to be dry, so don't plant it next to a leaking faucet or in a poorly drained corner. Like all acacias, it has spines on the branches. In the summer, 4-inch seed pods mature and hang in clusters. If you gather your own seed for this acacia, be careful not to take seed which is in a twisted pod or from a tree which is part of a thicket. Choose a tree with the biggest leaves you can find to avoid gathering seed that has been hybridized with the Gregg acacia, a species which is not so desirable.

75. Bigtooth Maple
Acer grandidentatum
Benny J. Simpson

75. Bigtooth Maple
Acer grandidentatum
Benny J. Simpson

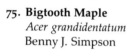

76. Chalk Maple
Acer leucoderme
Benny J. Simpson

120

75. **Latin Name** *Acer grandidentatum*
    A-ser gran-dee-den-TAY-tum
    Common Name BIGTOOTH MAPLE
    Height 50 feet
    Fall Color Reds
    Range Trans-Pecos, Edwards Plateau, Lampasas Cutplain, and
    mountains in New Mexico, Colorado, Idaho, and Oklahoma
    Part Sun
    Propagation Seed

Bigtooth
Maple
*Beautiful
Fall Colors*

The last week in October and first week in November, the bigtooth maples put on a show in the Guadalupe Mountains. They turn from gold to orange to red and finally to purple. The leaves seem to be illuminated by the sunshine. The result is truly spectacular. The leaves, 2–3 inches across, have deep indentions, making large tooth shapes, which give this maple its name. This tree should be very useful in our landscapes for several reasons. One, of course, is its magnificent fall color, as strong as the sweetgum. Also, it is healthy on our soils, not suffering from chlorosis. It is drought-resistant. And it is a wonderfully manageable size for city lots. Planted in an artistically natural drift of several trees, it could be a gorgeous sight in a park or in front of a civic building.

76. **Latin Name** *Acer leucoderme*
    A-ser loo-koe-DERM-ee
    Common Name CHALK MAPLE
    Height 20 feet
    Fall Color Gold to orange and red
    Range Sabine National Forest, southeastern United States
    Sun to Part Sun
    Propagation Seed

Chalk Maple
*Rare
in Texas*

Supposedly, when this tree gets old enough, its trunk gets white, giving it the name *leucoderme*, "white skin." This tree is winter-hardy and will grow in limestone soils. It is naturally small and graceful, and the leaves are velvety on the undersurface. In the fall, it turns lovely colors, ranging from golden yellow to deep red. Add all this together, and you have a very useful tree for landscaping. These trees are now available from Native Sun Nursery in Austin.

Texas
Buckeye
*Clusters
of Bloom a
Foot High*

77. **Latin Name**   *Aesculus arguta*
ESS-que-luss are-GUE-tuh
Common Name   TEXAS BUCKEYE
Height   Up to 35 feet
Bloom Time   March, April
Range   Edwards Plateau to Oklahoma and Missouri
Sun to Dappled Sun
Propagation   Seed as soon as ripe, right off the tree

The yellow and white flowers and green star-shaped leaves come out together very early in the spring when most trees are still bare. The flower clusters are like huge 1-foot candelabra. The buckeye seeds mature in June, usually in twos. They are about half an inch in size, dark brown with a white "eye." This tree is usually much smaller than 35 feet, more often 12–15 feet, if growing on a limestone outcropping. Because it is so small and well-shaped, it is very attractive for the small garden. It likes a little protection from the west sun, because its leaves are fairly large and thin and can scorch in a hot, dry summer. It needs watering during this period to stay looking its best. It's a good tree to have growing over groundcover or a shady garden because it doesn't seed out very much.

Scarlet
Buckeye
*Late Spring
Bloomer*

78. **Latin Name**   *Aesculus pavia* var. *pavia*
ESS-que-luss PAY-vee-uh variety PAY-vee-uh
Common Name   SCARLET BUCKEYE
Height   Up to 28 feet
Bloom Time   April to May
Range   Texas north to Illinois and east to Florida
Sun to Dappled Shade
Propagation   Seed

This buckeye is an understory tree. This means that it does very well in shady places under larger trees, as long as it gets enough sun at bloom time. Since it flowers rather late for an understory tree, it must be placed so that it gets the low slanting sun of early morning or very late evening. Or put it under a pecan tree, since pecans don't leaf out until early May. In the understory situation, *A. pavia* is often found with a curving trunk. With more sun, it grows upright, more like an ordinary tree. But the leaves might burn in late summer if not given lots of water. When healthy, the leaves of this tree make it lovely even when it is not in bloom, because they are such a pretty shape. When flowering, the stalks of red flowers cover the tree like scores of candelabra. It is a good tree to plant over groundcover, because it does not seed out much.

77. Texas Buckeye
Aesculus arguta
Julie Ryan

77. Texas Buckeye
Aesculus arguta
Dr. Geoffrey Stanford

78. Scarlet Buckeye
Aesculus pavia
Julie Ryan

78. Scarlet Buckeye
Aesculus pavia
Andy Wasowski

False Indigo, River Locust
Exotic Flowers

79. **Latin Name**   *Amorpha fruticosa* var. *angustifolia*
uh-MOR-fuh froo-tee-KOZE-uh variety an-gus-tee-FOLE-ee-uh
Common Name   FALSE INDIGO, RIVER LOCUST
Height   6–9 feet
Bloom Time   April, May
Range   Most of the United States
Sun to Part Sun
Propagation   Seed, cuttings, or layering

This graceful little tree is usually found growing with its roots in a stream or pond, but if you keep your lawn green, you should have no trouble keeping your amorpha happy. It grows both in limestone and in deep black soil. Keep it pruned to a maximum of five trunks. I love this tree because it is so small and graceful. If you have it planted over a flower bed or groundcover, cut off the bloom stalks (they will be easy to reach), so you won't have to weed out any seedlings. The flowers on 6–9-inch spikes can be an incredible deep royal purple with brilliant orange anthers. My favorite specimen seems to have fallen prey to a bulldozer, so I had to photograph this smaller, paler example. Obviously, this is a species that needs to have its most striking clones selected and propagated by cuttings or layering. Often people think of the name "leadplant" when they hear "amorpha." This refers to *A. canescens*, which has gray leaves, the color of lead. *A. texana*, endemic to Texas, is more drought-resistant.

Texas Madrone, Naked Indian Tree
Exquisite

80. **Latin Name**   *Arbutus xalapensis*
ar-BEW-tus sah-luh-PEN-sis
Common Name   TEXAS MADRONE, NAKED INDIAN TREE
Height   Up to 30 feet
Bloom Time   February to April (2 weeks)
Fall Color   Evergreen
Range   Edwards Plateau, Trans-Pecos, to Guatemala
Sun to Part Sun
Propagation   Seed off the tree planted within 24 hours

This is the most beautiful tree I have ever seen. It is sometimes multi-trunked; the trunks are a soft cream color, revealed by the exfoliating bark, which is a rich terra-cotta red gradually turning a chocolate brown. The leaves are a bright, smooth green. The blossoms in early spring are clusters of little white flowers. The fruits in fall look like ripe red raspberries hanging all over the tree in 3-inch clusters. This tree likes water, but not swamp conditions. It has been exceedingly difficult to transplant because its root system is similar to azaleas—not surprisingly, since it is in the azalea family. Unlike azaleas, it does not require an acid soil. In fact, Texas madrone can be observed growing on limestone. It needs a full year of very frequent watering before establishing a root system adequate for normal watering. The Agricultural Experiment Station in Dallas proved it both winter-hardy and able to take our heat.

79. False Indigo
Amorpha fruticosa
Andy Wasowski

80. Texas Madrone
Arbutus xalapensis
Walt Davis, DMNH

125

81. Button Bush
Cephalanthus occidentalis
Edith Bettinger

81. Button Bush
Cephalanthus occidentalis
Charles Finsley, DMNH

82. Texas Whitebud
Cercis canadensis
var. *texensis alba*
Benny J. Simpson

82. Texas Redbud
Cercis canadensis var. *texensis*
Julie Ryan

81. **Latin Name** *Cephalanthus occidentalis*
      seh-fuh-LAN-thus ox-uh-den-TAY-lis
      Common Name BUTTON BUSH
      Height Up to 18 feet, usually smaller
      Bloom Time June to September
      Range Eastern Canada to Florida and California
      Sun to Dappled Shade
      Propagation Seed
          Germination 30–40 days with no pretreatment

Button Bush
Blooms
All Summer

Though naturally found as 3-foot bushes in swamps and shallow lakes, in moist woods, or in watered yards, *Cephalanthus* can grow into a tree with a trunk up to a foot in diameter, but 8 feet is a more normal height. The more water the better, especially to get a profusion of the 1-inch balls of white-to-pink flowers that are so sweet that beekeepers report larger amounts of honey when *Cephalanthus* is nearby. Butterflies are also attracted. The nutlets are produced in September and October and are eaten by at least twenty-five species of birds, especially water fowl. The tree may be multi-trunked or single-trunked. The wood is brittle. I recommend this only for a well-watered yard or one by a stream or lake.

---

82. **Latin Name** *Cercis canadensis* var. *texensis*
      SER-sis kan-uh-DEN-sis variety tex-EN-sis
      Common Name TEXAS REDBUD
      Height 40 feet
      Bloom Time March, April
      Range Edwards Plateau, Cross Timbers, Blackland Prairies;
          Oklahoma
      Sun to Part Sun
      Propagation Seed or green cutting in the spring

Texas Redbud
A Thirty-Day
Bloomer

Texas redbud is marketed here as Oklahoma redbud and White Texas, the latter selected at Germany Nursery in Fort Worth. The redbud commonly found in our nurseries is the eastern redbud. Texas redbud differs in that it will grow on limestone and will thrive on 10 inches less rainfall a year. You can identify it at a nursery by its leaves, which are thicker, more rounded and less heart-shaped, and much shinier than those of the eastern variety. The Mexican redbud needs even less water than the Texas redbud. Its leaves are even smaller, crinkled, and woolly, which cuts down on evaporation. All these redbuds are winter-hardy. They tend to lose their leaves early, which can be an advantage if you want the autumn sun to warm your patio or sunroom. Both the Texas and Mexican redbud have learned to sucker, so you can have a multi-trunked tree. But you'll also have to prune. The white Texas redbud grows more slowly.

127

83. Desert Willow
Chilopsis linearis
Harold Laughlin

84. American Smoke Tree
Cotinus obovatus
Benny J. Simpson

84. American Smoke Tree
Cotinus obovatus
Benny J. Simpson

83.   **Latin Name** *Chilopsis linearis*
         KY-lop-sis lin-ee-ERR-is
        Common Name   DESERT WILLOW
        Height   Up to 30 feet
        Bloom Time   May, June, occasionally in summer and fall
        Range   West Central Texas to California
        Sun to Part Sun
        Propagation   Seed or cuttings in late summer

Desert
Willow
Ethereal

Prune off the lower branches of the *Chilopsis* and you'll wind up with one of our prettiest trees, with light, graceful foliage and orchid-like blossoms. The color of the blossoms varies from white to pink to lavender with purple in the throat. This little desert tree grows naturally by dry stream beds, where its roots can always find moisture. Though it is considered drought-resistant, it can appreciate water. Sometimes you will get dead twigs. Don't worry about it; the tree is fine. Just prune them out. It is highly tolerant to cotton root rot. The seed comes packed in long, thin beans. It germinates rapidly, but it is better not to transplant the seedling for a full year, because the roots are exceedingly fragile. A white strain and a rosy purple strain have recently been released to nursery growers, so in a few years these two should be available at your local nursery.

84.   **Latin Name** *Cotinus obovatus*
         ko-TINE-us o-boe-VAY-tus
        Common Name   AMERICAN SMOKE TREE
        Height   Up to 30 feet
        Bloom Time   April, May
        Fall Color   Orange and yellow
        Range   Edwards Plateau to Oklahoma, Missouri, Arkansas, and Tennessee
        Sun to Part Sun
        Propagation   Seed

American
Smoke Tree
Blossoms
Airy as Smoke

Obviously, the large, soft, hazy clouds of flowers give the tree its name. I had always heard that our native smoke tree was not as pretty as the European version. Not so! I think that our pink flowers are much more attractive than their yellowish-green ones. This little tree also has beautiful fall foliage—orange and gold, with some touches of red. Our smoke tree is highly drought-resistant. It should *never* be fertilized or over-watered; either will make it grow too rapidly, making the wood so brittle that small branches will break off in a wind. Use this tree in a very dry place in poor soil. A limestone hill is perfect.

85. Hawthorn
Crataegus reverchonii
Benny J. Simpson.

85. Hawthorn
Crataegus reverchonii
Benny J. Simpson

85. Hawthorn
Crataegus reverchonii
Andy Wasowski

86. Texas Persimmon
Diospyros texana
Benny J. Simpson

85. **Latin Name** *Crataegus reverchonii*
    kruh-TEAGUE-us rev-er-SHONE-ee-eye
    Common Name HAWTHORN
    Height 25 feet
    Bloom Time April
    Range Northeast Texas and adjacent Oklahoma
    Sun to Part Sun
    Propagation Seed or root cuttings in spring

Hawthorn
*Beautiful &
Delicious*

This tree is beautiful when in bloom. It is blanketed with shiny white blossoms. The bark is reddish and exfoliating, especially in the fall. Sometimes the trees are multi-trunked, as in the picture. In the autumn, the berries turn bright red and remain after the leaves have fallen, making another beautiful display. The berries don't remain all winter, because the birds devour them. Now, here comes the bad part. The insects also find the tree delicious. Worse yet, hawthorns, like apple trees, can carry the cedar-apple rust, a disease that affects junipers. It is a good tree for parks, or for the easygoing homeowner. The hawthorn requires a deep soil and watering, if planted on the uplands.

86. **Latin Name** *Diospyros texana*
    dye-OS-pear-us tex-ANE-uh
    Common Name TEXAS PERSIMMON
    Height 40 feet, but usually much smaller
    Sun
    Propagation Seed

Texas
Persimmon
A-Peeling Bark

This persimmon is much smaller than the common persimmon, and the fruits are smaller—only about an inch long. They are black and are much enjoyed by many birds and mammals. Texas persimmon grows in limestone, except down on the coast, where it gets its lime from oyster shells. There is no brilliant fall color, probably because this tree is evergreen in warm places like Brownsville. Further north, it loses its leaves in the autumn, but it is perfectly winter-hardy in all parts of West Texas, including the Panhandle. Its chief attraction is the beauty of its bark, which is white and peeling. The leaves—not pictured, since this photo was taken in February—are only 1–2 inches long, dark green, and leathery. The flowers are tiny and rather dull. Use this tree close to a window so you can enjoy its bark all year.

Possumhaw Holly, Deciduous Holly, Possumhaw
Cherchez la Femme

87. **Latin Name**   *Ilex decidua*
EYE-lex dee-SID-you-uh
Common Name   POSSUMHAW HOLLY, DECIDUOUS HOLLY, POSSUM-HAW
Height   30 feet, but usually much smaller
Range   East and Central Texas to Kansas to Virginia to Florida
Sun to Dappled Shade
Propagation   Seed, as soon as ripe

This looks very like the yaupon holly in the summer, but in the winter it loses its leaves, and the red berries become the main decoration. But be sure that you get a female tree, because the male is just plain bare all winter. When you buy your tree, check to see if there is a berry or blossom present. The berries (actually drupes) hold on until new leaves come out in the spring. The fruits are eaten by at least nine species of birds and seem to attract mockingbirds and waxwings, among others. Some trees have yellow instead of red fruits, and some have red fruits that gradually turn yellow. Barry Kridler of Mount Pleasant, Texas, has been working on producing a red drupe that keeps its color and a yellow one that is dependably yellow. In its home area, it is not necessary to plant a male for the female to produce berries. Chances are, there are enough in your neighborhood already, so your female will have no trouble getting pollinated. The female tree also seems capable of being pollinated by the common Burford hollies.

Yaupon Holly
Very Popular

88. **Latin Name**   *Ilex vomitoria*
EYE-lex vom-ee-TORE-ee-uh
Common Name   YAUPON HOLLY
Height   25 feet
Spacing   At least 15 feet
Fall Color   Evergreen
Range   East Texas bottomlands to Oklahoma, Florida, Virginia
Sun to Dappled Shade
Propagation   Seed and softwood cuttings

I wonder if this yaupon would be as well-liked if its rather graphic Latin name were better known! As it is, this tree is so popular because it is evergreen, drought-resistant, and healthy. According to its natural range, it shouldn't grow in caliche, but it does. Be sure to get a female if you want the red drupes in the winter. Buy one with a flower or a berry on it. (By the way, these drupes survive freezing very well and keep their bright red color. At least mine did, for which the mockingbirds were grateful.) Always give this tree a good pruning in the spring. Clean out all the branches on the inside. Never trim on the outside or you will destroy the proportions and grace, not to mention next winter's drupes. Shrubs have been developed from this tree. "Houston," no longer available, made a 3–5-foot hedge. The dwarf yaupon holly makes 1–2-foot mounds.

87. Possumhaw Holly
Ilex decidua
Benny J. Simpson

87. Possumhaw Holly
Ilex decidua
Andy Wasowski

88. Yaupon Holly
Ilex vomitoria
Julie Ryan

Ashe Juniper, Mountain Cedar
The "Cedars" of Cedar Hill

89. **Latin Name** *Juniperus ashei*
    joo-NIP-er-us ASH-ee-eye
Common Name ASHE JUNIPER, MOUNTAIN CEDAR
Height 18–30 feet
Bloom Time Late fall and winter
Fall Color Evergreen, blue berries
Range Missouri to Texas to Guatemala
Sun to Shade
Propagation Seed

Though usually called a "cedar," this tree is really a juniper. We have no native cedars. The shape of *J. ashei* is haphazard, in contrast to the cone-shaped top of *J. virginiana*, which grows alongside it in much of its range. Ashe juniper apparently does not carry the cedar-apple rust—a big advantage! The blue fruits are displayed at the ends of the branches of female trees, making the tree an attractive pale blue until the fruits are eaten. They are important to many small mammals and birds, including the cedar waxwing and the curved-bill thrasher. A rare bird, the golden-cheeked warbler, requires a whole grove of Ashe junipers for nesting. These trees may be like huge shrubs in full sun and when left unpruned; in the woods or on shady lots, they are tall and narrow. They are occasionally multi-trunked. The bark, reddish and shaggy when young, gets silvery and fluted with age. They have a wonderful aromatic scent in the winter time. Cut a branch and burn it down to the sparks in the fireplace, letting it waft through the house.

Alligator Juniper
Alligator Bark

90. **Latin Name** *Juniperus deppeana*
    joo-NIP-er-us dep-ee-ANE-uh
Common Name ALLIGATOR JUNIPER
Height 20–30 feet, rarely 50 feet
Fall Color Evergreen
Range Trans-Pecos to central Arizona and central Mexico
Propagation Seed

Alligator juniper is named for its bark, which actually resembles the back of an alligator. It is also sometimes called "checker-bark juniper." It is stout and strong, and occasionally has multiple and leaning trunks, which are very appealing. The branching starts fairly high on the trunk, so that there is little pruning involved and the attractive trunk is always exposed. It grows out of limestone and shallow soils and is extremely drought-resistant. The brown fruit stays on the tree two years before it is mature. This is one of our most beautiful junipers, with its evergreen foliage ranging from bright green to smoky-blue to silver-gray. Alligator juniper is winter-hardy at least as far north as Denton.

89. Ashe Juniper
Juniperus ashei
Dr. Geoffrey Stanford

89. Ashe Juniper
Juniperus ashei
Julie Ryan

90. Alligator Juniper
Juniperus deppeana
Benny J. Simpson

90. Alligator Juniper
Juniperus deppeana
Sally Wasowski

Wax Myrtle
A Bayberry

91. **Latin Name** *Myrica cerifera*
muh-RYE-kuh or MY-ruh-kuh ser-ee-FEAR-uh
Common Name WAX MYRTLE
Height 20 feet, rarely 40 feet
Bloom Time Blue-gray berries fall and winter
Fall Color Evergreen
Range East Texas to New Jersey
Sun to Dappled Shade
Propagation Seed, cuttings, layering

This evergreen shrub trims well into a small tree, more often 20 feet than 40 feet tall. It grows naturally by bodies of water, but will easily grow in areas receiving as little as 25 inches of rain a year. It does require a full year of watering after transplanting. The leaves are a light olive-green, spicy and aromatic when bruised. The berries, which line the branches on female trees only, are eaten by forty species of birds. If you boil the waxy blue-gray berries, you can make candles out of them. This tree will grow in acid, sandy loam; in black, sticky prairie soil; or in limestone. It does not seem to sucker like its cousin the dwarf wax myrtle.

Mexican Plum
Limestone
Plum

92. **Latin Name** *Prunus mexicana*
PROO-nus mex-ee-KANE-uh
Common Name MEXICAN PLUM
Height 25 feet
Bloom Time March
Range Kentucky to Texas to northeastern Mexico
Sun to Dappled Shade
Propagation Seed

The white blossoms of this plum are a perfect contrast to the hot pink of *Ungnadia* and redbud, because all these trees bloom about the same time and thrive in similar environments. Mexican plum will grow right out of limestone, but does equally well on blackland or sand. The plums are a little over an inch long. Many birds and smaller mammals love them. This makes an excellent understory tree, because it blooms before the taller trees leaf out. It is drought-resistant, but will grow more quickly with lots of water. It does not sucker and seems to be amazingly pest-free. In full sun it develops a beautiful spreading shape and casts very dense shade. The bark is exfoliating when young, but gets deeply furrowed when older, much different from the satiny bark of most plums and cherries.

91. Wax Myrtle
Myrica cerifera
Benny J. Simpson

91. Wax Myrtle
Myrica cerifera
Sally Wasowski

92. Mexican Plum
Prunus mexicana
Benny J. Simpson

92. Mexican Plum
Prunus mexicana
Dr. Geoffrey Stanford

137

93. Carolina Buckthorn
Rhamnus caroliniana
Benny J. Simpson

94. Eve's Necklace
Sophora affinis
Benny J. Simpson

94. Eve's Necklace
Sophora affinis
Sally Wasowski

93. **Latin Name** *Rhamnus caroliniana*
RAM-nus care-o-lin-ee-ANE-uh
Common Name INDIAN CHERRY, CAROLINA BUCKTHORN
Height 35 feet
Fall Color Yellow to orange
Range Trans-Pecos to North Carolina
Sun to Part Sun
Propagation Seed or softwood cuttings

Indian Cherry, Carolina Buckthorn

Shining Fall Foliage

This little tree should be grown for its glossy leaves and brilliant color in the fall. The ones growing on the blacklands have the glossiest leaves, but they need extra water during the summer. The ones growing in limestone are more drought-tolerant. Both produce little cherry-like drupes in late summer. Starting off a bright red, they gradually turn a shiny black as they mature, attracting several species of birds. Some people confuse this tree with viburnum. Check the leaves. If they alternate up the stem, you have found the *Rhamnus*. The trunk is smooth and sometimes blotched. Some branching occurs close to the ground, so prune until about a third of the trunk is exposed.

94. **Latin Name** *Sophora affinis*
suh-FORE-uh or SOFF-or-uh af-FIN-is
Common Name EVE'S NECKLACE, NECKLACE TREE, TEXAS SOPHORA
Height Up to 25 feet
Bloom Time June
Range Central Texas and adjacent Oklahoma and Louisiana
Sun to Part Sun
Propagation Seed as soon as ripe, softwood cuttings

Eve's Necklace, Necklace Tree, Texas Sophora

Pink Buds, Black Beads

The blooms look like pale pink wisteria. The seed pods give the tree its name, because they look like a necklace of black beads when they are dry. This tree will grow out of limestone and is extremely drought-tolerant. It usually grows naturally on the edge of woods, where it gets tall and thin, leaning out into the sun, shoulder to shoulder with other trees. Give it space and it will develop into a nicely shaped tree. The foliage does not grow thickly, so this is a good tree to have in the flower garden, where it can give light shade from afternoon sun. It is moderately fast-growing. When very young, it might freeze back to the ground in a hard winter, but the roots will be unaffected, and the tree will return the following spring, perhaps even suckering. If this happens, be sure to cut off stems you don't want until the tree is recovered.

95. Texas Mountain Laurel
Sophora secundiflora
Fort Worth Botanic Garden

95. Texas Mountain Laurel
Sophora secundiflora
Fort Worth Botanic Garden

96. Mexican Buckeye
Ungnadia speciosa
Dr. Geoffrey Stanford

96. Mexican Buckeye
Ungnadia speciosa
Dallas Museum of Natural History

95. **Latin Name** *Sophora secundiflora*
       suh-FORE-uh or SOFF-or-uh se-kune-di-FLORE-uh
    Common Name TEXAS MOUNTAIN LAUREL
    Height 20–30 feet
    Bloom Time April
    Fall Color Evergreen
    Range Texas coast to New Mexico and Mexico
    Sun
    Propagation Seed, scarified first if completely ripe

Texas
Mountain
Laurel
*A Laurel
Un-Hardy*

The purple wisteria-like blooms are very fragrant. The evergreen leaves are dark and shiny. Unless it is pruned, it is densely shrubby. It would make a very expensive hedge, however, because it grows so slowly. It suffered winter damage in Dallas–Fort Worth during the frozen Christmas of 1983. No trees died, but because of their slow growth rate, it will take them years to look attractive again. The seed pods are short, fat, and taupe-colored. The seeds are red and are often used to make jewelry. The Indians used them, powdered, in exceedingly small amounts, as a drug. They are poisonous to livestock and humans. The tree must be in a well-drained situation.

96. **Latin Name** *Ungnadia speciosa*
       oong-NOD-ee-uh spee-see-O-suh
    Common Name MEXICAN BUCKEYE
    Height 30 feet, but usually much smaller
    Bloom Time March, early April
    Fall Color Golden yellow
    Range Limestone soils of Texas, New Mexico, Mexico
    Sun to Part Sun
    Propagation Seed, while barely ripe, or with scarification

Mexican
Buckeye
*If You Can
Only Have
One . . .*

If you have space for only one tree, this is the one I would recommend. Mexican buckeye is the color of redbud, and the flowers cover the tree just as profusely, but it is better in every way. Its blossoms are much larger—about an inch—and prettier and have a delightful scent. The fruit looks like a three-seeded buckeye, though in fact it isn't a buckeye at all! The leaves are leathery, dark green, and lustrous. They stay on the tree until late in the fall, when they turn a lovely golden yellow. The bark is attractively mottled, very thin and smooth. It will take moist situations or extreme drought. It likes limestone best, but will grow in sand or clays. This little tree should be used extensively, because it will grow all over Texas and is healthy, drought-resistant, and especially beautiful.

141

97. Rusty Blackhaw Viburnum
Viburnum rufidulum
Benny J. Simpson

97. Rusty Blackhaw Viburnum
Viburnum rufidulum
Dr. Geoffrey Stanford

97. Rusty Blackhaw Viburnum
Viburnum rufidulum
Benny J. Simpson

Rusty
Blackhaw
Viburnum
*Best Viburnum
for Our Area*

97.   **Latin Name** *Viburnum rufidulum*
          vi-BURN-um rue-FID-you-lum
Common Name RUSTY BLACKHAW VIBURNUM
Height Up to 40 feet
Bloom Time April
Fall Color Gold and orange
Range Kansas to Virginia to Florida to Texas
Sun to Part Sun
Propagation Seed

This is a beautiful shrub or tree with glossy, dark leaves. Unpruned, at the edge of a lawn or driveway or wooded lot, it can form an elegant hedgerow. To use it as a tree, plant it in good sun and prune off the bottom branches. It needs no extra watering in Dallas, but would need some during the summer in more western parts of the state. There are tiny red hairs on the stalk of the leaf, giving this viburnum the name "rusty." Another source for the name might be the fact that the new leaves start off a bronzy red. In April, the flowers are 3-inch clusters of white, glistening against the shiny green leaves. Hanging clusters of shiny drupes gradually turn from pink to blue-black as they ripen during the summer.

Plants for Heavy Shade

TWO HOURS OF SUN OR DAPPLED SHADE

Plants for a Perennial Garden

Achillea millefolium   **Yarrow**
Aquilegia canadensis   **Wild Columbine**
Aquilegia longissima   **Longspur Columbine**
Cooperia drummondii   **Rain Lily**
Lobelia cardinalis   **Cardinal Flower**
Malvaviscus drummondii   **Turk's Cap**
Tradescantia spp.   **Spiderwort**

Naturalizing Plants

Cornus drummondii   **Rough Leaf Dogwood**

Shrubs and Decorative Trees

Callicarpa americana   **American Beauty Berry**
Ilex vomitoria   **Yaupon Holly**
Myrica cerifera   **Wax Myrtle**

Vines

Parthenocissus quinquefolia   **Virginia Creeper**

Plants for Light Shade

FOUR TO SIX HOURS OF SUN, MORNING
BEST, OR DAPPLED SHADE ALL DAY

Plants for a Perennial Garden

Achillea millefolium   **Yarrow**
Aquilegia canadensis   **Wild Columbine**
Aquilegia longissima   **Longspur Columbine**
Asclepius tuberosa   **Butterfly Weed**
Camassia scilloides   **Wild Hyacinth**
Chrysanthemum leucanthemum   **Ox-Eye Daisy**
Cooperia drummondii   **Rain Lily**
Coreopsis lanceolata   **Golden Wave**
Echinacea purpurea   **Purple Coneflower**
Echinocereus triglochidiatus   **Claret Cup Cactus**
Eupatorium coelestinum   **Blue Boneset**
Habranthus texanus   **Copper Lily**
Hesperaloe parviflora   **Red Yucca**
Hymenocallis liriosme   **Spider Lily**
Iris brevicaulis   **Louisiana Iris**
Lantana horrida   **Texas Lantana**
Lobelia cardinalis   **Cardinal Flower**
Malvaviscus drummondii   **Turk's Cap**
Melampodium cinereum   **Blackfoot Daisy**
Opuntia imbricata   **Walking Stick Cholla**
Opuntia phaeacantha   **Prickly Pear**
Pavonia lasiopetala   **Pavonia**

Penstemon cobaea   **Wild Foxglove**
Penstemon murrayanus   **Scarlet Penstemon**
Phlox divaricata   **Louisiana Phlox**
Physostegia praemorsa   **Lionheart (autumn)**
Physostegia pulchella   **Lionheart (spring)**
Ratibida columnaris   **Mexican Hat**
Rudbeckia hirta   **Black-Eyed Susan**
Salvia coccinea   **Scarlet Sage**
Salvia greggii   **Cherry Sage**
Solidago spp.   **Goldenrod**
Tradescantia spp.   **Spiderwort**
Verbena elegans var. *asperata*   **Hardy Verbena**
Vernonia baldwinii   **Ironweed**
Yucca pallida   **Pale Leaf Yucca**
Zexmenia hispida   **Zexmenia**
Zigadenus nuttallii   **Death Camas**

Naturalizing Plants

Cornus drummondii   **Rough Leaf Dogwood**
Eryngium leavenworthii   **Eryngo**
Gaillardia pulchella   **Indian Blanket**
Helianthus maximiliani   **Maximilian Daisy**
Monarda fistulosa   **Bergamont**

Prunus rivularis   **Creek Plum**
Rhus aromatica   **Aromatic Sumac**
Sambucus canadensis   **Elderberry**

Shrubs and Decorative Trees

Callicarpa americana   **American Beauty Berry**
Lonicera albiflora   **Honeysuckle Bush**

Aesculus arguta   **Texas Buckeye**
Aesculus pavia   **Scarlet Buckeye**
Arbutus xalapensis   **Texas Madrone**
Cercis canadensis   **Texas Redbud**
Crataegus reverchonii   **Hawthorn**
Ilex decidua   **Possumhaw Holly**

Ilex vomitoria   **Yaupon Holly**
Juniperus ashei   **Ashe Juniper**
Myrica cerifera   **Wax Myrtle**
Prunus mexicana   **Mexican Plum**
Rhus virens   **Evergreen Sumac**
Sophora affinis   **Eve's Necklace**
Ungnadia speciosa   **Mexican Buckeye**
Viburnum rufidulum   **Rusty Blackhaw Viburnum**

Vines

All vines

Plants for Later Spring Bloom

Plants for a Perennial Garden

Achillea millefolium   **Yarrow**
Amsonia ciliata   **Texas Blue Star**
Camassia scilloides   **Wild Hyacinth**
Chrysanthemum leucanthemum   **Ox-Eye Daisy**
Coreopsis lanceolata   **Golden Wave**
Delphinium virescens   **White Larkspur**
Echinacea purpurea   **Purple Coneflower**
Hesperaloe parviflora   **Red Yucca**
Hymenocallis liriosme   **Spider Lily**
Ipomopsis rubra   **Red Gilia**
Iris brevicaulis   **Louisiana Iris**
Melampodium cinereum   **Blackfoot Daisy**
Opuntia imbricata   **Walking Stick Cholla**
Opuntia phaeacantha   **Prickly Pear**
Penstemon cobaea   **Wild Foxglove**
Penstemon murrayanus   **Scarlet Penstemon**
Phlox divaricata   **Louisiana Phlox**
Phlox drummondii   **Drummond's Phlox**
Physostegia pulchella   **Lionheart**
Salvia farinacea   **Mealy Blue Sage**
Thelesperma filifolium   **Greenthread**
Tradescantia spp.   **Spiderwort**
Verbena bipinnatifida   **Prairie Verbena**
Verbena elegans var. *asperata*   **Hardy Verbena**
Yucca pallida   **Pale Leaf Yucca**
Yucca thompsoniana   **Thompson Yucca**
Zigadenus nuttallii   **Death Camas**

Naturalizing Plants

Callirhoe involucrata   **Winecup**
Cornus drummondii   **Rough Leaf Dogwood**
Engelmannia pinnatifida   **Cut-Leaf Daisy**
Gaillardia pulchella   **Indian Blanket**
Oenothera missouriensis or *O. rhombipetala*   **Yellow Evening Primrose**
Oenothera speciosa   **Pink Evening Primrose**
Rhus glabra   **Smooth Sumac**
Sambucus canadensis   **Elderberry**

Shrubs and Decorative Trees

Berberis swaseyi   **Texas Barberry**

Acacia wrightii   **Wright Acacia**
Aesculus pavia   **Scarlet Buckeye**
Amorpha fruticosa   **False Indigo**
Cotinus obovatus   **American Smoke Tree**
Sophora affinis   **Eve's Necklace**
Sophora secundiflora   **Texas Mountain Laurel**

Shade Trees

Magnolia grandiflora   **Southern Magnolia**
Sapindus saponaria   **Soapberry**

Vines

Bignonia capreolata   **Crossvine**
Campsis radicans   **Trumpet Vine**
Clematis pitcheri   **Leatherflower**
Lonicera sempervirens   **Coral Honeysuckle**
Passiflora incarnata   **Passion Flower**

Plants for Fall Bloom

Plants for a Perennial Garden

Cooperia drummondii   **Rain Lily**
Eupatorium coelestinum   **Blue Boneset**
Habranthus texanus   **Copper Lily**
Hibiscus coccineus   **Texas Star Hibiscus**
Lantana horrida   **Texas Lantana**
Liatris spp.   **Gayfeather**
Lobelia cardinalis   **Cardinal Flower**
Machaeranthera tanacetifolia   **Tahoka Daisy**
Malvaviscus drummondii   **Turk's Cap**
Melampodium cinereum   **Blackfoot Daisy**
Pavonia lasiopetala   **Pavonia**
Physostegia praemorsa   **Lionheart**
Ratibida columnaris   **Mexican Hat**
Salvia coccinea   **Scarlet Sage**
Salvia farinacea   **Mealy Blue Sage**
Salvia greggii   **Cherry Sage**
Solidago spp.   **Goldenrod**
Tradescantia spp.   **Spiderwort**
Verbena bipinnatifida (if watered all summer)   **Prairie Verbena**
Verbena elegans var. *asperata*   **Hardy Verbena**

Vernonia baldwinii   **Ironweed**
Zexmenia hispida   **Zexmenia**

Naturalizing Plants

Eryngium leavenworthii   **Eryngo**
Gaillardia pulchella (if watered all summer)   **Indian Blanket**
Helianthus maximiliani   **Maximilian Daisy**
Monarda fistulosa   **Bergamont**

Shrubs and Decorative Trees

Anisacanthus wrightii   **Flame Acanthus**
Chilopsis linearis   **Desert Willow**

Vines

Campsis radicans   **Trumpet Vine**
Ipomoea quamoclit   **Cypress Vine**
Maurandya antirrhiniflora   **Snapdragon Vine**

Plants That Are Green
in the Winter

Plants for a Perennial Garden

Achillea millefolium (groundcover) **Yarrow**
Aquilegia canadensis **Wild Columbine**
Chrysanthemum leucanthemum
  (groundcover) **Ox-Eye Daisy**
Cooperia drummondii (above 15° F) **Rain Lily**
Coreopsis lanceolata (groundcover) **Golden
  Wave**
Echinocereus triglochidiatus **Claret Cup Cactus**
Habranthus texanus (above 20° F) **Copper Lily**
Hesperaloe parviflora **Red Yucca**
Iris brevicaulis **Louisiana Iris**
Opuntia imbricata **Walking Stick Cholla**
Opuntia phaeacantha **Prickly Pear**
Verbena elegans var. *asperata* (above
  20° F) **Hardy Verbena**
Yucca (all) **Yucca**

Naturalizing Plants

Callirhoe involucrata **Winecup**

Shrubs and Decorative Trees

Berberis swaseyi **Texas Barberry**

Berberis trifoliolata **Agarito**
Leucophyllum frutescens (gets thin) **Cenizo**
Lonicera albiflora **Honeysuckle Bush**

Arbutus xalapensis **Texas Madrone**
Ilex vomitoria **Yaupon Holly**
Juniperus ashei **Ashe Juniper**
Juniperus deppeana **Alligator Juniper**
Myrica cerifera **Wax Myrtle**
Rhus virens (above 15° F) **Evergreen Sumac**
Sophora secundiflora (above 15° F) **Texas
  Mountain Laurel**

Shade Trees

Magnolia grandiflora **Southern Magnolia**
Quercus fusiformis **Escarpment Live Oak**
Quercus pungens var. *vaseyana* **Vasey Oak**
Quercus virginiana **Coast Live Oak**

Vines

Bignonia capreolata **Crossvine**
Gelsemium sempervirens **Carolina Jessamine**
Lonicera sempervirens (gets thin) **Coral
  Honeysuckle**

SHADY PERENNIAL GARDEN

Many people have heard that if you have a sprinkler system you will rot out native plants or that they *need* to have full sun. The homeowner living in an old house on a shady street with a lovely St. Augustine lawn might think that there is nothing in this book for such a yard. This plan shows that you can have a lovely, lush evergreen look in a shady yard with native plants. The advantage is that you can have this look with something blooming each season and water only one to two hours a week in the summer.

This yard is on a gentle slope. The limestone rough-cut rock near the street is a wall built two rocks high to retain the soil. The west boundary is a brick wall with rough cedar railing above to form a retaining wall for the higher courtyard beyond. The shade trees shown are huge old trees which almost meet each other. To be this size, they are probably older than you are, so you didn't get to choose them. In this dream plan I could, so I chose trees which, with the exception of the oaks, would be ideal, because they do not give you a lot of seedlings to weed out. The sunlight is dappled shade with part sun in different spots according to the hour and the season. The smaller decorative trees are all blooming or evergreen.

Nearly everything against the brick wall is evergreen, and many of the plants in the flower bed are green in the winter, so that this yard is attractive all year long. All trees should be pruned high on the trunk with three exceptions. The wax myrtle (*Myrica cerifera*) should be allowed to grow fairly low to the ground, because few things would grow in the dense shade under it and behind the chinquapin oak (*Quercus muhlenbergii*). The yaupon holly (*Ilex vomitoria*) should be pruned the same way for the same reason, since it is behind the Shumard oak. The *Rhus virens* in this instance is being used as a shrub rather than a tree and should be pruned accordingly. The Carolina jessamine (*Gelsemium sempervirens*) will spill over the fence, making a sheet of yellow in early spring and being evergreen the rest of the year. If you like, you can let it form a groundcover under the madrone (*Arbutus xalapensis*). The pavonia is bare while the bulbs are blooming. When the bulbs' foliage is dying back, the pavonia will get big and green and bloom until frost.

It is very dry under a bois d'arc (*Maclura pomifera*). The Louisiana irises are at the place on the slope where the most water will collect, but they still might need an occasional extra watering to stay fresh all summer. The big flower garden will take two years to get thick and lush. After first frost, cut back the dead stalks to

147

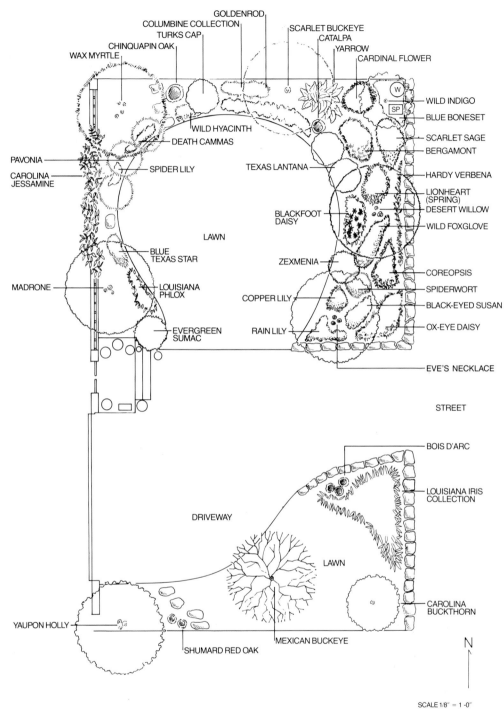

GOLDENROD
COLUMBINE COLLECTION
TURKS CAP
CHINQUAPIN OAK
WAX MYRTLE
SCARLET BUCKEYE
CATALPA
YARROW
CARDINAL FLOWER

W
SP

WILD INDIGO
BLUE BONESET
SCARLET SAGE
BERGAMONT
HARDY VERBENA

WILD HYACINTH
DEATH CAMMAS
PAVONIA
CAROLINA
JESSAMINE
SPIDER LILY
TEXAS LANTANA
LIONHEART
(SPRING)
DESERT WILLOW
WILD FOXGLOVE

BLACKFOOT
DAISY

LAWN

BLUE
TEXAS STAR
ZEXMENIA
COREOPSIS
SPIDERWORT
MADRONE
LOUISIANA
PHLOX
COPPER LILY
BLACK-EYED SUSAN
EVERGREEN
SUMAC
RAIN LILY
OX-EYE DAISY

EVE'S NECKLACE

STREET

BOIS D'ARC

LOUISIANA IRIS
COLLECTION

DRIVEWAY

LAWN

CAROLINA
BUCKTHORN

YAUPON HOLLY

N

SHUMARD RED OAK
MEXICAN BUCKEYE

SCALE 1/8" = 1 -0"

Shady Perennial Garden

about 2 inches and let the dead leaves collect and form a mulch for the winter. There will be islands of green and scatterings of small green rosettes. These and the graceful trunks of the decorative trees will make the garden look attractive and full of promise for the summer. Beginning in early March, the rosettes will start to get big. Gradually, things will begin to bloom, starting with the Mexican buckeye (*Ungnadia speciosa*). There will be a big burst of color in May, which will continue through June. July and August will always have something colorful, but there will be another big show in October, which will continue until frost.

Cultivated woods on a city lot. Trees include American elm, cedar elm, red oak, Ashe juniper, pecan, red juniper, bois d'arc, hackberry, white ash, and Texas ash. The groundcover is English ivy.

Sally Wasowski

7

Shade Trees

Тhese are the huge trees that take years to reach maturity. They are planted to the south and west to shade a house or patio from the fierce summer sun. They are used similarly to shade offices and to provide shade for parking. Most of these trees are deciduous, which means that they drop their leaves in the fall. This is an advantage, because then the bare branches let in the winter sun to help warm the building.

It is best to plant these trees during the cooler months while they are dormant. We get some of our best rains during the winter, and the sun does not dry out the ground. The cool, moist soil promotes root growth. Another advantage is that the tree does not lose water due to evaporation through the leaves. Even so, water your tree one hour at a time, once a week in the winter. Deep watering is important to encourage the roots to go deep. Otherwise, the tree is totally dependent on your watering and has not developed drought resistance. Also, it is so shallow-rooted that it could easily be blown down in a storm. The roots are close to the surface, where they can damage foundations, sidewalks, and patios. Suckers will try to grow from sections of exposed roots.

These trees look most handsome when they are pruned out fairly high on the trunk. This lets the sunshine reach the ground, so that grass and groundcover can be planted underneath.

**Caddo Maple,
Sugar Maple**
*Plant for
Fall Color*

98. **Latin Name** *Acer saccharum*
A-ser sah-KAR-um
Common Name   CADDO MAPLE, SUGAR MAPLE
Height   100 feet
Fall Color   Gold to orange and red
Range   Eastern half of United States and Canada
Sun
Propagation   Seed sown as soon as ripe

Many northern transplants (people, that is) complain that one of the worst things about living in Texas is that they miss seeing maple trees—especially in the fall. Once you get out of the sands of East Texas, we have three good maples that do not get chlorosis (iron deficiency). Two are in the decorative tree section, because they are small trees. The Caddo maple (of maple syrup fame) is large. The fall color is more often golden than red. Still, even a northerner must admit it is a beautiful fall display. Being a maple, it is a handsome tree, with attractively shaped leaves and those distinctive winged fruits, called "samaras." The wings are important, because they enable the seed to fly through the air on the wind, making new Caddo maples in other areas. This tree will grow in limestone and blackland soils and will grow as far west as Fort Worth with no supplemental watering.

Pecan
*The State
Tree of Texas*

99. **Latin Name** *Carya illinoinensis*
CARE-ee-uh ill-e-noy-NEN-sis
Common Name   PECAN
Height   150 feet
Range   Central and Northwest Texas to Indiana and Alabama
Propagation   There are many improved varieties of pecan trees on the market these days, and I'd recommend buying one rather than planting a seed

The pecan is a giant, towering over most of the other trees in this book. In a yard, it can ultimately provide shade for most of your home and make life a bit easier for your air conditioner. Some people are rapturous about the pecan tree, especially its nuts. Other folks despise it! For one thing, it tends to drop dead limbs a lot, smashing flowers, getting in the way of the lawn mower, littering the patio, and so forth. Then, too, it *does* seem to have more than its fair share of afflictions: galls, twig girdlers, aphids, borers, weevils. Pecan scab, which ruins the nuts, is a serious problem in humid areas. Tent caterpillars, or web worms, are not only the most unsightly, but very destructive. Within a week of emerging, they will have completely defoliated the entire host-branch. Show these invaders no mercy. Cut off the attacked branch and place it and the web on your driveway, break open the web, pour on some lighter fluid, toss on a lighted match, and stand back! If you per-

98. Caddo Maple
Acer saccharum
Andy Wasowski

98. Caddo Maple
Acer saccharum
Benny J. Simpson

99. Pecan
Carya illinoinensis
Sally Wasowski

99. Pecan
Carya illinoinensis
Julie Ryan

form this necessary surgery before the worms leave the web and find new homes (usually in the rest of your tree), I've found that your tree is usually free of them for two to three years. This method is far more effective and less costly than spraying poisons.

Catalpa, Cigar Tree, Catawba
A Touch of the Tropics

100. **Latin Name** *Catalpa bignonioides*
     kuh-TALL-puh big-none-ee-OID-ees
     Common Name CATALPA, CIGAR TREE, CATAWBA
     Height Up to 60 feet
     Bloom Time April, May (1 week)
     Range Florida to Louisiana, naturalized in East Texas, Oklahoma, and Arkansas
     Propagation Seed

This tree projects a tropical appearance with its huge, heart-shaped leaves and beautiful, orchid-like blossoms. The flowers drop to the ground still fresh, so they are delightful for children to play with and string into necklaces. The beans, or "cigars," start to get long and noticeable about a month after the flowers fall. They grow all summer and ripen in October. Though many thin seeds are packed into each bean (and the tree is loaded with beans, as you can see from the picture), seedlings under the tree are a rarity. The tree is tall and thin and gives sparse shade. These characteristics make it very desirable to use in a space where you want to grow a garden underneath. The problem with the catalpa is that it needs a lot of water. I do not recommend using this tree where you will see it all summer and fall unless you can provide it with plenty of moisture. Without it, the leaves go limp, get scorched, and turn yellow very early in the fall. Also, little limbs die back; they make the tree look messy and litter the ground.

Texas Ash
The Dry Ash

101. **Latin Name** *Fraxinus texensis*
     FRAX-suh-nus tex-EN-sis
     Common Name TEXAS ASH
     Height 50 feet
     Fall Color Gold to orange
     Range Arbuckle Mountains of Oklahoma, Central Texas and Edwards Plateau
     Propagation Seed

Texas ash is one of our prettiest fall trees. It grows shaped like a flame. Then it turns gold from the center, gradually gaining oranges, and is red at the very tips. It should be planted extensively instead of the Arizona ash. The Arizona ash came from an arid region, so it was naturally assumed to be drought-tolerant. It isn't. It grows in those arid regions only in stream beds. Texas ash is closely related to the white ash, which lines our streams in North Central Texas, but it will also grow on limestone and on the upland soils, making it our only drought-resistant ash. It is a fairly fast-growing tree, healthy and long-lived, with strong, hard wood.

100. Catalpa
Catalpa bignonioides
Julie Ryan

100. Catalpa
Catalpa bignonioides
Julie Ryan

101. Texas Ash
Fraxinus texensis
Sally Wasowski

155

102. **Sweetgum**
Liquidamber styraciflua
Andy Wasowski

102. **Sweetgum**
Liquidamber styraciflua
Sally Wasowski

103. **Bois d'Arc**
Maclura pomifera
Benny J. Simpson

103. **Bois d'Arc**
Maclura pomifera
Sally Wasowski

102. **Latin Name**   *Liquidamber styraciflua*
     lik-wid-AM-bur stye-rass-ee-FLUE-uh
     Common Name   AMERICAN SWEETGUM
     Height   150 feet
     Fall Color   Reds, with shadings of orange and purple
     Range   Connecticut to the mountains of Mexico
     Sun
     Propagation   Seed

American
Sweetgum
Chlorotic

Sweetgum will not grow at all well on limestone. When you see it in areas where limestone bedrock is only a few feet down, the tree gets chlorosis as soon as its roots make contact. The leaves turn yellow. This indicates severe iron deficiency. The full-length portrait shows not fall color, but chlorosis. Sweetgum should be grown only on sandy, acid soils. It also likes lots of water, and it is not considered drought-tolerant, especially in the early years. It is grown in limestone areas despite all these difficulties because it is such a beautiful red in the fall. The 1-inch sweetgum balls are spiky and painful to step on, but are often painted and used for decorations. About twenty-five species of birds eat the fruits. Sweetgum is fast-growing and long-lived. Buy your tree in the fall so you can choose your time and color for the fall foliage. Some turn later than others, and the leaves may be frozen and fall before turning red.

---

103. **Latin Name**   *Maclura pomifera*
     mack-LURE-uh pom-IFF-er-uh
     Common Name   BOIS D'ARC, OSAGE ORANGE
     Height   60 feet
     Bloom Time   April
     Range   Missouri to eastern half of Texas
     Propagation   Root cuttings, softwood cuttings, seed

Bois d'Arc,
Osage Orange
Mammoth Food?

There are lots of good stories about bois d'arc. Strong and supple, the wood was used by the Osage Indians for their bows. The fruit was eaten by some Indians; bois d'arc trees grow at the base of Indian cliff-dwellings in Arizona, theoretically sprouted from left-over dinners. The wood, which never seems to rot, was once used in pier-and-beam construction. I've heard that after an old house is moved off its bois d'arc piers, the piers sprout leaves! Charles Finsley, a curator at the Museum of Natural History in Dallas, suggests that the bois d'arc must have developed in tandem with a beast like the mammoth. "Look at all those bois d'arc apples!" he says. "Something big *must* have eaten them for there to be so many." The tree is very stout and tough and grows in any kind of soil (even out of limestone), in creek beds or as fencerows in dry fields. The roots are bright orange and the wood is orange or yellow underneath the bark. I'd choose a male bois d'arc. It's covered with greenish-white lacy flowers in April, and there are no bois d'arc apples. The "apples" are supposed to repel roaches, but, unhappily, I have found no evidence to support that theory. The name "horse apple" seems to be more accurate—horses love them!

157

104. Southern Magnoli
Magnolia grandiflor
Benny J. Simpson

104. Southern Magnolia
Magnolia grandiflora
Sally Wasowski

105. Honey Mesquite
Prosopis glandulosa
Sally Wasowski

105. Honey Mesquite
Prosopis glandulosa
Dr. Geoffrey Stanfor

158

104. **Latin Name**   *Magnolia grandiflora*
       mag-NOLE-ee-uh gran-dee-FLORE-uh
   Common Name   SOUTHERN MAGNOLIA
   Height   50 feet, rarely to 135 feet
   Spacing   30 feet
   Bloom Time   May, occasionally in summer
   Fall Color   Evergreen
   Range   South and East Texas to North Carolina
   Propagation   Seed

Southern
Magnolia
Stately

Magnolia has class—large, dark, glossy evergreen leaves, huge, thick-petaled, creamy white flowers up to 9 inches across, and bright red seeds. The flowers smell strongly of lemon. Since it grows naturally in acid sands, it is surprising that magnolia grows on limestone, but it does very well there, as long as it has enough water. Unpruned, the branches grow down to the ground, the whole tree being pyramidal in shape. The roots are up near the surface of the soil, and the leaves prevent both sun and rain from reaching the ground. If you have the space and the choice, it is best not to prune. Sometimes the trees are pruned high on the trunk. When they are, it is necessary to prune high enough so that sufficient sunlight can reach the base for groundcover to grow. It is better to buy a selected variety instead of a seedling. That will guarantee that you get a well-shaped tree with larger leaves and prolific blooms. "Majestic Beauty" is very good for our area.

---

105. **Latin Name**   *Prosopis glandulosa*
       pruh-SO-pis glan-due-LOW-suh
   Common Name   HONEY MESQUITE
   Height   20–50 feet
   Bloom Time   May, occasionally to September
   Range   Kansas to Louisiana to New Mexico
   Sun
   Propagation   Seed

Honey
Mesquite
*A Lovely
Shade Tree*

This mesquite does not sucker, but the root system is wide and deep, greedily seeking available water. Give plenty of water to the lawn or garden growing underneath, because the tree takes a lot of water out of the soil. The branches are thorny, which discourages grazing. When little branches die and fall out of the tree, they need to be picked up off the grass, because the stickers on them can damage lawn mower tires. The flowers are yellow and sweet-smelling. The seed pods are nutritious, eaten by horses, cattle, and goats—not to mention quail, squirrels, deer, and white-winged dove. I especially like this tree because the leaves are so thin and lacy, catching every breeze and providing a light, dappled shade, under which lawns or gardens can grow and bloom. This is the best shade tree for a small yard.

OAKS

The cradle of our American oaks is in central Mexico. All of the approximately 250 species in the Western hemisphere can trace their lineage directly back to that land. Of all the states in the union, Texas claims the greatest diversity of oaks—forty-three species and two varieties, by some expert accounts. (But I won't go to the wall over that number.)

It is hard to identify a species of oak accurately, because the leaves may vary considerably, even on a single tree. Scholars get very technical and also very heated about the subject. There is a wonderful, and very likely apocryphal, tale about the renowned Professor Asa Gray of Harvard (1810–1888), who asked each student in his class to gather an oak leaf for identification. Five of his students impishly got samples off the same big tree just outside the door. From them, Gray identified five "new species." The only accurate way to identify an oak is by knowing where it grew—and by the acorns and leaves, which is why the individual oak pictures are of both leaves and acorns.

There are two main categories of oaks: the black oaks and the white oaks. The black oaks include all those which get fall colors, such as *Quercus shumardii* and *Quercus texana*. They usually have acorns which take two years to mature. In September, there is a big acorn which is ripe, and tiny acorns which will be mature the following year. If you lift the cap off the acorn, you will see that it is hairy inside. The name "black" was given because the bark on these trees is supposedly darker than on the other oaks. The black oaks occur only in North America. The white oaks include all the pin oaks and the live oaks. There are nineteen varieties of live oak in Texas, thirteen of them occurring only west of the Pecos River. The caps of their acorns are smooth inside, as in all white oaks. Live oaks are so named because the leaves stay green all winter. In April, the old leaves drop as new ones form, giving the tree a thin look for a week or so. Therefore, live oaks are not evergreen in the strict sense, but that is the easiest way to convey the fact that they will be green in the winter.

One way to reduce the ultimate size of your oak is to let it form multiple trunks. *Quercus shumardii* and *Quercus texana* are especially attractive with multiple trunks. The most common way to achieve this is to cut off the main stem at ground level when it is small and let three trunks come up and remain. Don't do this to the live oak (*Quercus virginiana*)—it may die! All oaks will sucker (send up baby trees from the roots) to some extent. If the new shoots are cut or mown off, they are usually no problem. Oaks are

Shumard Red Oak
Quercus shumardii
Dallas Museum of Natural History

106. Escarpment Live Oak
Quercus fusiformis
Benny J. Simpson

107. Lacey Oak
Quercus glaucoides
Benny J. Simpson

162

very fine trees, slow-growing, long-lived, the premier shade trees.

To plant your own oak from an acorn, first choose an oak tree you particularly like that grows near you. If you want an oak for red fall color, wait until the trees turn and get an acorn from the reddest one. That will not guarantee that your oak will be red, but the chances are increased. The acorn is ripe when it will easily snap out of the cup. Always gather your acorn directly off the tree. As quickly as you can, plant it where you want it to grow. Keep it moist if it will be over twelve hours before you can plant it.

---

106. **Latin Name** *Quercus fusiformis*
     KWER-kus fuse-ee-FORM-us
     Common Name ESCARPMENT LIVE OAK
     Height 36 feet
     Fall Color Evergreen
     Range Limestone outcrops from the Gulf to the Pecos, south to Mexico, north to the Red River and Oklahoma
     Sun

Escarpment Live Oak
Petite Live Oak

Many prefer to list this as a variety of *Q. virginiana*, the coast live oak. *Fusiformis* refers to the acorns, which are fusiform or spindle-shaped. The advantages of this live oak are that it is small, drought-resistant, and will grow on limestone. It is highly colonial, forming groves called oak mottes. Plant it only in a lawn where it is easy to mow off the suckers, or in the corner of a big lot where a grove would look nice.

---

107. **Latin Name** *Quercus glaucoides*
     KWER-kus glaw-KOY-dees
     Common Name LACEY OAK
     Height About 50 feet
     Fall Color Yellow-rimmed leaves
     Range Limestone escarpments in the Edwards Plateau and north-eastern Mexico
     Sun

Lacey Oak
Blue-Green Leaves

This is a moderate-sized tree, which can be made smaller and even more attractive by making it multi-trunked. The Lacey oak is grown mostly for the lovely blue-green of its leaves. It is drought-tolerant and grows on limestone. All of the oaks listed here have been proven to be winter-hardy for the North Central Texas area.

163

108. Bur Oak
Quercus macrocarpa
Benny J. Simpson

109. Chinquapin Oak
Quercus muhlenbergii
Benny J. Simpson

110. Vasey Oak
Quercus pungens var. *vaseyana*
Benny J. Simpson

108. **Latin Name**   *Quercus macrocarpa*
     KWER-kus mack-row-CAR-puh
     Common Name   BUR OAK
     Height   150 feet
     Fall Color   Brown
     Range   Central Texas north to New Brunswick and Saskatchewan
     Sun

Bur Oak
Impressively
Large

This majestic oak will seemingly grow anywhere, certainly anywhere in Texas. It is the most widely adaptive oak in the world. In the Midwest, it is called the "prairie oak," because it will quickly take over a fallow field in the prairies. The further south it grows, the bigger the acorns are, attaining a length of 2 inches in Texas. It is sometimes called "mossy-cup oak," because of the mossy fringe around the edge of the acorn cup. Although attaining its greatest size in the bottomlands, it will grow in the uplands and on limestone, and is very drought-resistant. It is reasonably fast-growing.

109. **Latin Name**   *Quercus muhlenbergii*
     KWER-kus mule-en-BURGE-ee-eye
     Common Name   CHINQUAPIN OAK (CHINK-uh-pin)
     Height   60 feet
     Fall Color   Brown
     Range   Well-drained uplands, Mexico to Canada
     Sun

Chinquapin
Oak
Looks Like
an Easterner

It is because of its leaves that this oak is named after the chinquapin, a tree native to the eastern United States. Many northeasterners will be reminded of the American chestnut. It is a very beautiful tree, with its large, dark green leaves giving it a lusher look than you'll find with other oaks. It is drought-resistant, though not as much so as the bur oak. It is tall and slender in shape, not so wide-spreading as most oaks.

110. **Latin Name**   *Quercus pungens* var. *vaseyana*
     KWER-kus PUN-jens variety vase-ee-A-nuh
     Common Name   VASEY OAK
     Height   35 feet
     Fall Color   Evergreen (almost)
     Range   Dry limestone hills in Southwest Texas
     Sun

Vasey Oak
A Live Oak
for Patios

In North Central Texas, Vasey oak will be completely evergreen only in mild winters, but you can count on it being *mostly* evergreen, unless there's a particularly bad freeze. Its advantage is that it is a comfortable size for our modern homes and yards. It is kin to the scrub oaks and extremely drought-tolerant.

111. Shumard Red Oak
Quercus shumardii
Benny J. Simpson

112. Texas Red Oak
Quercus texana
Benny J. Simpson

113. Coast Live Oak
Quercus virginiana
Benny J. Simpson

111. **Latin Name** *Quercus shumardii*
     KWER-kus shoe-MARD-ee-eye
     Common Name SHUMARD RED OAK
     Height 120 feet
     Fall Color Red
     Range Central Texas to Pennsylvania and Florida
     Sun

Shumard
Red Oak
*The Large
Red Oak*

Shumard red oak does well in our heavy clay soils and in limestone. It usually turns red every fall, whether we have a cold snap or not. A word of warning—it is best to select yours in the fall when the leaves are actually turning. While most of the Shumards sold in nurseries *will* turn the brilliant red you want, a few will not.

---

112. **Latin Name** *Quercus texana*
     KWER-kus tex-ANE-uh
     Common Name TEXAS RED OAK
     Height 35 feet maximum
     Fall Color Red
     Range Dry uplands in Central Texas and Edwards Plateau
     Sun

Texas
Red Oak
*The Small
Red Oak*

Texas red oak is often small enough to be mistaken for a shrub—around 10–15 feet tall. Even growing in a creek bed, it does not attain much of a towering presence. Its leaves are similar to the Shumard oak, and it differs mostly in that it is smaller and probably more drought-tolerant. It is the only red oak that occurs naturally on the Edwards Plateau west of Kerrville. The fall color is a beautiful red.

---

113. **Latin Name** *Quercus virginiana*
     KWER-kus ver-gin-ee-ANE-uh
     Common Name COAST LIVE OAK
     Height 60 feet
     Fall Color Evergreen
     Range Texas Gulf Coast to Atlantic, up the coast to Virginia
     Sun

Coast
Live Oak
*Our Familiar
Live Oak*

Though it prefers wet, warm sands, this live oak has adapted to heavy clay soils, limestone, and colder winters. It seems to change its size and leaves drastically under different soil conditions, so it is sometimes divided into many different species, but few of these are now considered valid. A general rule is: the drier the soil and the less of it covering the limestone, the smaller the tree will be.

Western Soapberry
A Tree for Every Season

114. **Latin Name**   *Sapindus saponaria* var. *drummondii*
sap-IN-dus sap-o-NARE-ee-uh variety druh-MUN-dee-eye
Common Name   WESTERN SOAPBERRY
Height   30 feet, rarely 50 feet
Bloom Time   Late May and early June (2 weeks)
Fall Color   Golden yellow
Range   Kansas to Louisiana to Mexico to New Mexico
Propagation   Seed

Both the male and the female soapberry have clusters of lovely white blossoms in the spring. The male is actually a little showier, with larger flowers. In the fall, the leaves turn a lovely pumpkin yellow. All winter, the golden berries are framed against a blue Texas sky, dropping just a week before the spring flowers appear. The translucent cover of the berries contains saponin, a substance which lathers in water. The pioneers used them to wash woolens. The berries are still used in Mexico as a laundry soap. The chinaberry has similar berries, except that they are opaque. It is in the *Melia* family and is native to Asia. The flowers are purple and bloom a month earlier. The leaves are much fancier, having many extra indentations. It is generally a shorter, broader tree, with brittle wood, and is not considered to be as desirable as the soapberry here, but it is highly prized in other parts of the world, where it is known as "Indian lilac." The soapberry can sucker when it is young, but if you keep the suckers cut off, they will eventually stop. Seedlings are not numerous.

Bald Cypress
Old Baldy

115. **Latin Name**   *Taxodium distichum*
tax-O-dee-um DIS-tick-um
Common Name   BALD CYPRESS
Height   Up to 130 feet
Range   Swampy ground, Massachusetts to Florida to Texas
Propagation   Seed, hardwood cuttings

This is a conifer that is deciduous; in the fall the leaves turn a soft brown and drop from the tree. Some bald cypress have lived to be 1,200 years old. These trees have a trunk diameter of 8 feet. This is the same cypress you'd find in the Florida Everglades. It is an ancient tree—a remnant of dinosaur days, when it grew widely in mighty forests with the sequoia, now native only in isolated pockets in California, and the ginkgo, once thought to be extinct until rediscovered on a mountain top in Asia. Though a swamp tree, bald cypress has been found to be remarkably drought-tolerant after it has become well established. It is now very uncertain that its famous "knees" are for breathing in the swamps, because it also grows knees in the desert! It has been rapidly gaining in popularity recently as a park planting, especially around lakes, but it is also appearing in private yards. It has been in cultivation in Europe since 1640. It seems to have no preference for acid sands or for limestone, growing equally well on both. Though not naturally at home on black prairie land, it seems to be doing well there.

114. Soapberry
Sapindus saponaria var. *drummondii*
Sally Wasowski

114. Soapberry
Sapindus saponaria var. *drummondii*
Harold W. Hoffman, DMNH collection

115. Bald Cypress
Taxodium distichum
Andy Wasowski

169

116. **Latin Name** *Ulmus americana*
ULL-mus uh-mer-ee-KANE-uh

American Elm
Quick Shade

Common Name AMERICAN ELM
Height 70–120 feet
Fall Color Yellow
Range Eastern third of Texas, eastern two-thirds of United States
Propagation Seed

This is one of the best trees to plant if you want a lot of shade in a hurry. American elm has vase-shaped branching which makes it very identifiable, except when side by side with the Siberian elm. If you're planning to live a long life, it is important not to get these confused. The Siberian (Chinese, Asiatic) elm usually gets diseased and dies in about 50 years, while the American elm has been known to live 300 years and more. It is susceptible to Dutch elm disease, a fungus which wiped out the elms in the Midwest and Northeast a number of years ago, but that does not seem to be a big problem in Texas. The seeds are small, less than half an inch long, and flat, which is good, because a bumper crop is produced every spring; a larger seed would make it harder to weed out the seedlings in your groundcover or garden. The root system is rampant and heavy, taking on sidewalks, flower beds, and sewer systems—and winning.

---

117. **Latin Name** *Ulmus crassifolia*
ULL-mus krass-ee-FOLE-ee-uh

Cedar Elm
Individualistic

Common Name CEDAR ELM
Height 90 feet
Fall Color Yellow to gold
Range New York to Kansas to Texas
Propagation Seed in spring

I love cedar elms because each has its own shape. They are irregular, more tall than broad, with slightly drooping branches, and tiny stiff leaves. You can always tell a cedar elm for sure if you try to rub a leaf the wrong way; it is very rough. Julie describes the leaves in the fall as little golden coins floating down. The bark is also very rough, with corky projections on the trunks of very small, nursery-sized trees. Sometimes they get corky wings on the twigs and branches. Unlike those of other elms, the seeds ripen and spread in the fall—which is apparently not as advantageous as in the spring—because you usually don't have to weed out a lot of cedar elms. They grow quickly and get very big in swamps, but they also grow in dry limestone soils and take heat reflected by pavement. This is a relatively fast-growing tree, tough and healthy, and it should be used more often than it is. Another good elm is the winged elm (*Ulmus alata*), which gets to be about 60 feet tall and, like the cedar elm, is not very dense. It is also extremely healthy and fairly fast-growing, probably the better elm for people living on sandy soils.

116. American Elm
Ulmus americana
Sally Wasowski

116. American Elm
Ulmus americana
Julie Ryan

117. Cedar Elm
Ulmus crassifolia
Julie Ryan

117. Cedar Elm
Ulmus crassifolia
Sally Wasowski

Plants for Early Spring Bloom

Plants for a Perennial Garden

Aquilegia canadensis **Wild Columbine**
Aquilegia longissima **Longspur Columbine**

Naturalizing Plants

Prunus rivularis **Creek Plum**
Rhus aromatica **Aromatic Sumac**

Shrubs and Decorative Trees

Berberis trifoliolata **Agarito**
Lonicera albiflora **Honeysuckle Bush**

Aesculus arguta **Texas Buckeye**
Arbutus xalapensis **Texas Madrone**
Cercis canadensis **Redbud**
Crataegus reverchonii **Hawthorn**
Prunus mexicana **Mexican Plum**
Ungnadia speciosa **Mexican Buckeye**
Viburnum rufidulum **Rusty Blackhaw Viburnum**

Vines

Gelsemium sempervirens **Carolina Jessamine**

Plants for Fall Foliage

RED

Naturalizing Plants

Cornus drummondii **Rough Leaf Dogwood**
Rhus lanceolata and *R. glabra* **Sumac**

Shrubs and Decorative Trees

Acer grandidentatum **Bigtooth Maple**

Shade Trees

Liquidamber styraciflua **Sweetgum**
Quercus shumardii **Shumard Oak**
Quercus texana **Texas Red Oak**

Vines

Parthenocissus quinquefolia **Virginia Creeper**

YELLOW

Shrubs and Decorative Trees

Acer leucoderme **Chalk Maple**
Cotinus obovatus **American Smoke Tree**
Rhamnus caroliniana **Carolina Buckthorn**
Ungnadia speciosa **Mexican Buckeye**
Viburnum rufidulum **Rusty Blackhaw Viburnum**

Shade Trees

Acer saccharum **Caddo Maple**
Fraxinus texensis **Texas Ash**
Quercus glaucoides **Lacey Oak**
Sapindus saponaria **Soapberry**
Ulmus americana **American Elm**
Ulmus crassifolia **Cedar Elm**

MAKE YOUR OWN WOODS

Sometimes people just want shade and privacy from their yard. A woods is ideal for that. In a woods, the trees are not given the space to develop their full potential and most desirable shape. They are tall and thin, struggling for light. There are typically at least three stories or layers of growth in a woods.

The first level is a high canopy of big shade trees. These are the biggest circles on the plan, the trees that you should plant first. Buy the largest you can, 4-inch caliper or bigger if you can afford it. (Caliper is the diameter of a tree's trunk 4–5 feet up from the ground.)

The middle level in a woods is called the understory. These are small decorative trees or immature large trees. Since you are making your own woods, this is your chance to have all the beautiful blooming trees positioned so that they get sun before the shade trees leaf out. Your woods will be a cloud of pink and white in the spring. Then, for the fall, plant those trees which turn a beautiful color, so that your woods will be a glory of reds and yellows. Position these so that they can catch the sun when leaves are on the shade trees, because leaves turn color better in the sun.

The third level is the undergrowth, which makes a groundcover in a new woods where there is a fair amount of light on the forest floor. The ground is covered with leaf mold in more mature woods. For a more finished look, plant groundcover under the trees. I would use *Vinca major* or English ivy because they are evergreen, but if you want to stay all native, use the Virginia creeper (*Parthenocissus quinquefolia*). If you want a cultivated look, maintenance should be twice a year. In April or May, clean out all the saplings, grasses, Japanese honeysuckle, poison ivy, and anything else that you don't want. (If you are wondering how you could get all that stuff in your very own woods that you carefully planted yourself, I can tell you in one word: birds.) In December after the leaves have fallen, trim off any vines that are growing up the trees. Do not rake the leaves. They are valuable as mulch and return nutrients to the soil.

Buried in the midst of the woods are several *Juniperus ashei*. These give structure to the woods. They provide privacy in the winter and offer a foil of green to set off the spring color and make the fall colors even more vivid.

For a wilder look, plant flowers on the edge of the woods. Make your choices from the lists for Light Shade or Heavy Shade. If you

173

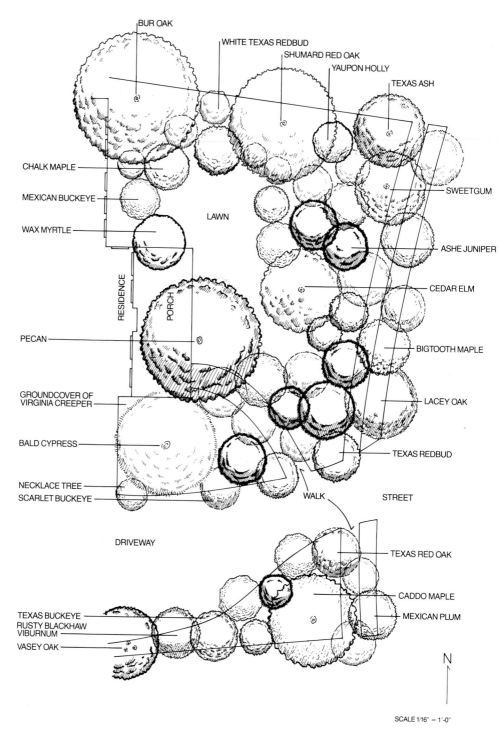

BUR OAK
WHITE TEXAS REDBUD
SHUMARD RED OAK
YAUPON HOLLY
TEXAS ASH
CHALK MAPLE
MEXICAN BUCKEYE
WAX MYRTLE
LAWN
SWEETGUM
ASHE JUNIPER
RESIDENCE
PORCH
CEDAR ELM
PECAN
BIGTOOTH MAPLE
GROUNDCOVER OF
VIRGINIA CREEPER
LACEY OAK
BALD CYPRESS
NECKLACE TREE
SCARLET BUCKEYE
TEXAS REDBUD
WALK
STREET
DRIVEWAY
TEXAS RED OAK
CADDO MAPLE
MEXICAN PLUM
TEXAS BUCKEYE
RUSTY BLACKHAW
VIBURNUM
VASEY OAK

N

SCALE 1/16" = 1'-0"

Make Your Own Woods

live on the hills around Austin or some similar dry and rustic place with no sidewalks and no clear boundaries, use only the trees on the Especially Drought-Tolerant list and let the local grasses be the groundcover. Here, again, you could plant wildflowers, if you wish, on the sunny edge of your woods.

A cascade of coral honeysuckle in the spring for the hummingbirds flying north.

8

Vines

I've tried to include a good cross section of the vines you might be most likely to want in your garden. There's one to bloom at every time of the year. Three are evergreen and one has brilliant fall color. In general, vines like their roots in a cool, shady spot and climb into a sunny place to bloom. The Virginia creeper (*Parthenocissus quinquefolia*) will take lots of shade; the trumpet vine (*Campsis radicans*) will take the most sun and reflected heat.

I did not get into the grapevines, because I think that's a book in itself. Very briefly, from the grapevines that I have observed, they seem to hybridize freely among themselves and with anything domestic that comes along. They are strong, healthy, aggressive, accommodating as to sun or shade, and drought-resistant. The grapes are thick-skinned and vary from vine to vine, depending on soil, ancestry, and weather.

Crossvine
Evergreen

118. **Latin Name** *Bignonia capreolata*
     big-NONE-ee-uh kap-ree-o-LATE-uh
Common Name CROSSVINE
Spacing At least 4 feet
Bloom Time April, May
Range Southeastern United States
Perennial Evergreen
Sun to Part Sun
Propagation Seed or softwood cuttings

Anytime you have something evergreen, it is valuable, with the exception of Japanese honeysuckle, of course, which overcomes everything in its path. Crossvine climbs by means of tendrils, so if you want it to climb a wall, give it a pattern of wire to cling to. The odor of the flowers is considered fragrant by some, unpleasant by others. This is in the same family as *Chilopsis* and *Catalpa*, two trees pictured in this book. Crossvine is most closely related to trumpet vine (*Campsis radicans*), but is not nearly so rambunctious. It is easy to control. If it gets too big, prune it after flowering. This crossvine is already in the nursery trade. It will grow on limestone soils, blacklands, and sands. It will definitely need watering in the summer.

Trumpet Vine
Pros & Cons

119. **Latin Name** *Campsis radicans*
     KAMP-sis RAD-ee-kans
Common Name TRUMPET VINE
Spacing 6 feet
Bloom Time May to October
Range Eastern half of Texas and United States
Perennial
Sun to Part Sun
Propagation Seed, very easy at any time

Trumpet vine blooms all summer and attracts hummingbirds. It also attracts ants, which swarm inside the flowers and prevent them from being used as centerpieces on your dinner table. Unlike *Bignonia capreolata*, it is deciduous. As soon as the leaves drop in autumn, cut back the canes to the woody trunk, because they always die over the winter and are harder to cut later when dry or intermixed with next year's growth. Also, this is a good way to keep your trumpet vine in bounds. If you have the time, it is also a good idea to cut off the seed pods before they ripen. Each long "bean" is packed with seed, and you will have enough trouble controlling the suckers without worrying about seedlings as well. In other words, *Campsis* is so healthy, so drought-resistant, so well adapted to soils that it can become a pest. *Campsis* climbs by aerial rootlets which attach themselves to any surface. The canes have a way of forcing themselves into tight places, such as under your shingles, and then growing fat and damaging your roof. Plant it away from your house. "Madame Galen" is a variety which is more restrained, but does not bloom as profusely.

118. Crossvine
Bignonia capreolata
Benny J. Simpson

119. Trumpet Vine
Campsis radicans
Benny J. Simpson

Leatherflower
Non-aggressive

120. **Latin Name** *Clematis pitcheri*
KLEM-ah-tis PITCH-er-eye
Common Name LEATHERFLOWER
Spacing 2 feet apart
Bloom Time April to September
Range Edwards Plateau and the coast, north to Nebraska
Perennial
Part Sun or Dappled Shade
Propagation Seed or softwood cuttings

This is a small, weak, twining vine, climbing by tendrils. Give it a spot where its roots get some protection from the sun, on the north or east side of a fence or wall, or under a tree. It requires watering in the summer. It will need wire, a trellis, or a fence with spaces between the verticals for it to climb. It should be planted near your house or walkway, because you have to get close to it to enjoy it. It never blooms profusely, but there are usually delicate flowers throughout the summer. Colors range from purple to brick red. The autumn fruits are as conspicuous as the flowers, being fluffy balls of seed. Scarlet clematis (*C. texensis*) is very similar in culture and appearance. The flowers appear on the current year's growth, so do all your pruning, if needed, in fall or very early spring.

Carolina Jessamine
Winter-Blooming

121. **Latin Name** *Gelsemium sempervirens*
jel-SEE-mee-um sem-per-VYE-rens
Common Name CAROLINA JESSAMINE
Spacing 6 feet apart
Bloom Time January to April
Range East Texas to Florida and Virginia
Perennial Evergreen
Sun to Part Sun
Propagation Seed or softwood cuttings

This vine, which you can find in any nursery, is one of the best. It is evergreen, healthy, and will grow on any soil. The spectacular blooming is around March, when the vine is covered with fragrant yellow flowers. It is always timed perfectly for the early spring migration of hummingbirds. All summer and fall, there are usually no flowers, though occasionally you'll find one or two. Around Christmas, if the weather is mild, there is often a secondary blooming. Carolina jessamine (not jasmine) climbs by twining, so it needs wire or some other support to grow up. I've been told that if it is not near a tree in the wild, it will form a groundcover. It grows vigorously, so it will need several prunings during the growing season if you want it to stay tidy. Trim any suckers severely, or they can get out of hand in later years. It is readily available from your area nursery.

180

120. Leatherflower
Clematis pitcheri
Dr. Werner W. Shultz, DMNH collection

121. Carolina Jessamine
Gelsemium sempervirens
Benny J. Simpson

122. Cypress Vine
Ipomoea quamoclit
Harold Laughlin

123. Coral Honeysuckle
Lonicera sempervirens
Dr. Geoffrey Stanford

182

122. **Latin Name**   *Ipomoea quamoclit*
           eye-poh-MEE-uh KWAM-o-clit
      Common Name   CYPRESS VINE
      Spacing   1–4 feet
      Bloom Time   July to November
      Range   Southeastern United States and tropical America
      Annual
      Sun to Part Sun
      Propagation   Seed

Cypress Vine
A Morning
Glory

This atypical morning glory keeps its flowers open all day. It is a vigorous grower and reseeds itself pretty dependably. When only a few inches high, it starts flowering and blooms profusely all summer until frost. Being an annual, it can provide the cover you need in one growing season, and you don't have to worry about winter-hardiness. Another advantage is that the dry seeds never produce the mess a juicy-fruited vine can. The term "cypress" comes from the shape of the leaves, which make a thin, delicate haze of green. You could start a debate over whether or not this vine is a true Texas native. It might have been found once in Brazos County; all of the wild cypress vines might be escapees, some of them even hybrids. Commercial seed is available, but it is not always easy to find. To keep your cypress vine pretty until frost, plan to water it in the summer. For earlier flowering, you can start it inside and set it out in April.

123. **Latin Name**   *Lonicera sempervirens*
           lon-ISS-er-uh sem-per-VYE-rens
      Common Name   CORAL HONEYSUCKLE
      Spacing   3 feet apart
      Bloom Time   April, May, occasionally thereafter
      Range   East Texas to Nebraska and Maine to Florida
      Perennial Evergreen
      Sun to Dappled Shade
      Propagation   Hardwood cuttings and layering both very easy

Coral
Honeysuckle
Spring Food
for
Hummingbirds

Coral honeysuckle is a cascade of 2- to 3-inch-long tubes of red and orange every spring, just in time for the northward migration of the hummingbirds. The rest of the year it is attractive green foliage with an occasional flower, though it becomes less evergreen the further north you go. In Dallas, it gets a little thin in the coldest part of the year. If you put it in a pot and place it inside by a sunny window, it will bloom all winter. In its leaf structure, it greatly resembles *L. albiflora*, which is a shrub. Coral honeysuckle is a vigorous grower and bloomer in full sun, covering fences in a single growing season. In shade, it is a timid, graceful little thing. It climbs by twining, so it needs something to twine around. Like a few plants that grow beautifully in limy soils, it is not particularly drought-resistant. It can get scorched leaves in the summer if it does not get either watering or shade. It is usually easy to find in the nursery.

124. Snapdragon Vine
Maurandya antirrhiniflora
Julie Ryan

125. Virginia Creeper
Parthenocissus quinquefolia
Julie Ryan

124. **Latin Name** *Maurandya antirrhiniflora*
     ma-RAN-dee-uh an-teer-rin-ee-FLORE-uh
     Common Name SNAPDRAGON VINE
     Spacing 1–2 feet
     Bloom Time Mid-June to frost
     Range South Texas to California and Mexico
     Perennial
     Sun to Dappled Shade
     Propagation Sow seed in early spring

*Snapdragon
Vine
Very
Delicate*

During the summer, the tiny blue flowers are too small to be very impressive from a distance, but they are delightful close up with their snapdragon appearance. The vine is usually root-hardy as far north as Denton and McKinney. In the winter, the bare stems are covered with tiny brown spheres, which are the seed cases. The seed is not released until early spring. Whether the vine wintered-over or had to be grown from seed, it starts blooming in mid-June. It climbs by twining. The ivy leaves are delicate and less than an inch long. This vine grows well in a pot, up another plant, or in a hanging basket. Fine fish line makes an adequate trellis. Because it is so delicate, it can grow over a rose or among other plants, and not overpower them. As cool weather approaches, the blooms become more numerous. If you take it inside to a sunny window, it will bloom all winter. Then, gradually, set it out on mild days to harden it off before setting it outside for the spring.

---

125. **Latin Name** *Parthenocissus quinquefolia*
     par-thuh-no-SIS-us kwin-kuh-FOLE-ee-uh
     Common Name VIRGINIA CREEPER
     Spacing 6 feet
     Fall Color Red
     Range Texas to Florida to Minnesota
     Perennial
     Sun to Shade
     Propagation Seed, layering, cuttings

*Virginia
Creeper
Good Shady
Groundcover*

Quinquefolia means "five-leaved." That's not a bad thing to remember—it's one way you can tell this vine from poison ivy, which is three-leaved. The stem's aerial rootlets fasten themselves to trees or to masonry houses. It looks beautiful on a house, lush and green all spring and summer, brilliant red in the fall, and with black berries which the birds enjoy in the winter. It climbs strongly, and unless you have a stout house and can prune it off your roof, it could do damage. It is so vigorous that I have even seen it fighting it out with Japanese honeysuckle and holding its own. It can make a shady groundcover in a natural area, but don't let it climb your favorite trees, because it can weaken them just as English ivy does. In heavy shade, the fall color is often a dull pink instead of red. Poor sandy soils make this vine pleasantly healthy rather than aggressive. It is definitely drought-resistant. A cousin of Boston ivy, it is sometimes found with seven leaflets, or even six, instead of five.

126. Passion Flower
Passiflora incarnata
Dr. Geoffrey Stanford

Passion Flower, Maypop
Spectacular & Unique

126. **Latin Name** *Passiflora incarnata*
pass-sih-FLO-ruh in-kar-NAY-tuh
Common Name PASSION FLOWER, MAYPOP
Spacing 3 feet apart
Bloom Time May to August
Range Eastern third of Texas to Virginia and Florida
Perennial
Sun to Part Sun
Propagation Seed or cuttings

These flowers are 2½–3 inches across and unbelievably intricate. Some people place religious significance on the flower; the name "passion flower" refers to the passion of Christ. The vine is not particular as to soils or water. Nurseries carry some that look just like this, but are hybrids from Brazil, which are supposed to be marginally winter-hardy as far north as the Red River. *P. caerulea*, the species from Brazil, looks like our maypop and is hardy enough to have naturalized in some parts of the state. It is even evergreen in mild winters in sheltered places. If well-established, it can become rampant. The vines climb by tendrils, so they'll need support if you want to keep them off the ground. The flowers close at night, but they can make a wonderful daytime table arrangement, especially if you put a drop of paraffin in the center to keep them open longer. The yellow, egg-shaped fruits are mostly seed.

Plants for Summer Bloom

Plants for a Perennial Garden

Asclepius tuberosa **Butterfly Weed**
Eustoma grandiflorum (if started
  indoors) **Texas Bluebell**
Hibiscus coccineus **Texas Star Hibiscus**
Lantana horrida **Texas Lantana**
Machaeranthera tanacetifolia **Tahoka Daisy**
Melampodium cinereum (if watered) **Blackfoot
  Daisy**
Pavonia lasiopetala **Pavonia**
Ratibida columnaris **Mexican Hat**
Rudbeckia hirta **Black-Eyed Susan**
Salvia farinacea **Mealy Blue Sage**
Salvia greggii **Cherry Sage**
Tradescantia spp. **Spiderwort**
Verbena bipinnatifida **Prairie Verbena**
Verbena elegans var. *asperata* **Hardy Verbena**
Vernonia baldwinii **Ironweed**
Zexmenia hispida **Zexmenia**

Naturalizing Plants

Gaillardia pulchella (if watered) **Indian
  Blanket**
Monarda fistulosa **Bergamont**

Shrubs and Decorative Trees

Leucophyllum frutescens **Cenizo**
Cephalanthus occidentalis **Button Bush**
Chilopsis linearis (if watered) **Desert Willow**

Vines

Campsis radicans **Trumpet Vine**
Clematis pitcheri **Leatherflower**
Ipomoea quamoclit **Cypress Vine**
Maurandya antirrhiniflora **Snapdragon Vine**
Passiflora incarnata **Passion Flower**

MEXICAN PATIO GARDEN

Here is a plan for a townhome with very limited space. To shield the French doors from all-day summer sun, the quickest way to provide shade is with a pergola. This is a light wooden framework for vines, which instantly converts your patio into an outdoor room. Cypress vine (*Ipomoea quamoclit*) is an annual, so it grows quickly enough to provide shade the first summer, while not obstructing the winter sun which warms your home.

The patio is unmortared to prevent drainage problems and to make watering the vines on the pergola easy or optional. The 6-foot-high stuccoed walls give more immediate privacy than a slow-growing hedge. They also provide shade for the roots of plants located against the north and east sides. The south and west facing walls store heat for the night, giving protection to plants that might be hurt by a bad freeze if they were out in the open. The garden is low-upkeep, since there is no grass to mow and very little weeding once the plants are well established. The only plants that require regular watering are grouped around the fountain—the two hibiscus and the pot plants. They are placed on the pea gravel patio, so you can bury the pots in the gravel to ground level. This keeps the roots cooler and gives them a chance to go on down into the ground, so they are less dependent on your watering. The plants chosen for the pots are extremely drought-hardy shrubs, which bloom off and on all summer.

The fountain puts moisture into the air and cools the patio. This is an ancient trick that the Moors introduced to Spain. There is archaeological evidence that water gardens were popular in biblical times in the Middle East, where Moorish culture originated. The Spanish, of course, brought this custom to Mexico. The rest of the garden will look better and benefit from weekly waterings, but unless we have a drought, nothing will die if you forget once in a while, provided it has gotten established first.

For this plan, there is an emphasis on those plants which bloom a long time or which bear close inspection. Mexican buckeye (*Ungnadia speciosa*) is one of the best. Not only does it have spectacular bloom in the spring, but it turns a beautiful golden yellow in the fall. It is the perfect size for a garden this small. Texas mountain laurel (*Sophora secundiflora*) is one of our prettiest evergreen trees—with small, glossy leaves and lovely, fragrant blossoms; but it is cold-sensitive, so it needs the corner which absorbs the southwest sun and gives it protection from a north wind. The honey mesquite (*Prosopis glandulosa*) is the obvious choice for a

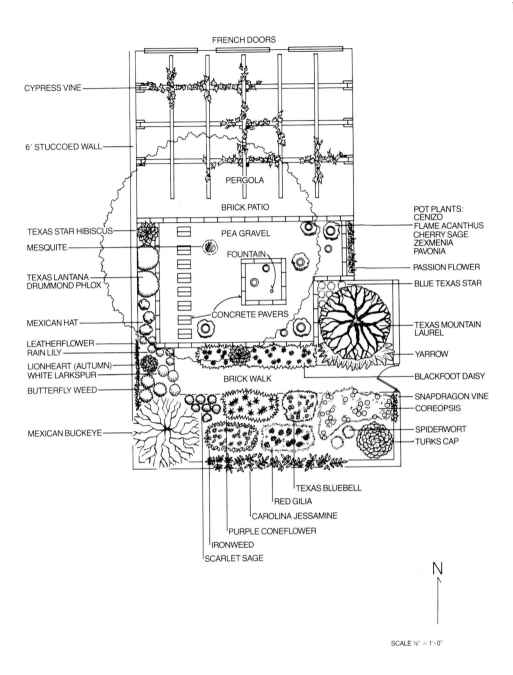

FRENCH DOORS

CYPRESS VINE

6' STUCCOED WALL

PERGOLA

BRICK PATIO

POT PLANTS:
CENIZO
FLAME ACANTHUS
CHERRY SAGE
ZEXMENIA
PAVONIA

TEXAS STAR HIBISCUS

PEA GRAVEL

MESQUITE

FOUNTAIN

PASSION FLOWER

BLUE TEXAS STAR

TEXAS LANTANA
DRUMMOND PHLOX

CONCRETE PAVERS

TEXAS MOUNTAIN
LAUREL

MEXICAN HAT

YARROW

LEATHERFLOWER
RAIN LILY

BLACKFOOT DAISY

LIONHEART (AUTUMN)
WHITE LARKSPUR

BRICK WALK

SNAPDRAGON VINE

BUTTERFLY WEED

COREOPSIS

SPIDERWORT

MEXICAN BUCKEYE

TURKS CAP

TEXAS BLUEBELL

RED GILIA

CAROLINA JESSAMINE

PURPLE CONEFLOWER

IRONWEED

SCARLET SAGE

N

SCALE ⅛" = 1'-0"

Mexican Patio Garden

189

shade tree because it is fast-growing and a good size for this yard, and its shade is light enough to let you fill all the space under it with flowers.

The vines are an important way of filling the walls with green and color in the small amount of space available to you. All of these vines climb by twining or tendrils, so they will require inconspicuous wires attached to the wall or a natural wood trellis for support. The clematis (*C. texensis*) has red flowers. The little *Maurandya* has tiny blue flowers. It is so delicate that if it covers the wall and also climbs over the coreopsis, you won't mind. The passion flower might get more vigorous, especially with the west wall for warmth in the winter. It sometimes suckers, so it is contained by the patios. You will also be glad to be able to walk over to inspect the flowers, which are extravagant and exotic. The Carolina jessamine (*Gelsemium sempervirens*) will be in its glory in early spring, but you will be most grateful to it all winter, because it fills the back wall with green.

Tawny Indiangrass covers a slope of Penn Prairie near Cedar Hill in fall.

The Vanishing Prairie

W HAT, you may wonder, is a chapter on prairie doing in a book on landscaping with native plants? Introduced to nature's original Blackland Prairie landscape, one wonders if that freedom, variety, and ability to thrive with limited rainfall could be translated to created landscapes. The question is raised by botanists, ecologists, preservationists, and landscape architects. A few people have begun to experiment to find out. You can, too.

In considering possible landscapes based on prairie, the starting place must be the prairie in its natural condition—not the easiest thing to find. Undisturbed native prairie is dwindling year by year. After the sad prospect of the vanishing prairie, we'll take a hopeful look at the prospect of prairie everywhere in home and public landscapes—a dream that could become reality, in time.

Let's take a trail walk through the tall-grass prairies and back over a hundred years into the past, when they seemed limitless. Our resources are the trailblazers before us, a shelf of books from the scant prairie sources of North Texas libraries—and a hungry eye for the horizon and the thousands of plants and animals that lie within its bounds.

My hope is that readers who are intrigued by the beauty and resource conservation that prairie-influenced landscapes seem to promise will explore further on their own, and perhaps even decide to join in the experimental gardening going on around the state. It's a new field (pardon the pun), and nature's creation, the prairie, is our best teacher.

J. Pope wrote in an 1854 report to the U.S. Congress on exploration for a route for the Pacific Railroad from the Red River to the Rio Grande:

> by far the richest and most beautiful district of country I have ever seen, in Texas or elsewhere, is that watered by the Trinity and its tributaries. Occupying east and west a belt of one hundred miles in width, with about equal quantities of prairie and timber . . . a gently undulating surface of prairie and oak openings, it presents the most charming views . . . a prospect of groves, parks, and forests, with intervening plains of luxuriant grass, over which the eye in vain wanders in search of the white village or the stately house, which alone seem wanting to the scene.

When you visit the prairie, time stops. Nature's rhythmic cycles reign there, as they have for millennia. Limitless space erases the constraint within us of being always bounded by walls, fences, barriers. Even in prairies as small as 15 acres, there is a spacious feeling that hints at the thrill the vast original prairie must have given.

The tall-grass Blackland Prairie of Texas once covered 12 million acres, a triangle of rich black land extending from Grayson, Fannin, Lamar, and Red River counties in northeast Texas southward to the San Antonio area, as well as two oblong "islands" that lie just to the east parallel to the Waco–San Antonio axis. It was a continuation of the Blackland Prairie that once extended northward through the plains states into southern Canada. In Texas, the mid-grass Grand Prairie that parallels the Blackland Prairie just to the west survived settlement better, because it is less tempting farmland. Both areas are important agriculturally today. There are other notable prairie ecosystems in Texas, such as the Coastal Prairies. Of the original Blackland Prairie area, less than 1 percent survives today. The islands of undisturbed Blackland Prairie that remain are a repository of ancient tall-grass lands as they were in prehistoric times. Like other relict prairies, they are a time capsule to the past, a biological baseline for agricultural experimentation, and a refuge of many beautiful wildflowers seen nowhere else in such variety and profusion.

Early European explorers and settlers didn't know what to make of the tall-grass prairie. They had never before seen such an ocean of waving grass. Diaries of early arrivals to the Midwest speak of riding for days with nothing in view but grass from horizon to horizon, dotted with an occasional tree. The scarcity of trees, except along stream beds, prompted some to conclude that the prairie was poor farmland. This notion was dispelled after farmers settled and broke the sod, finding the soil deep and rich and more easily cleared than eastern timber land. By 1920, it was "bounded and gutted," writes rangeman Clarence Bunch.

By the turn of the century, midwestern scientists theorized that the prairie was not an accident of nature, but the culmination of an evolutionary process that began when the Rocky Mountains first thrust up from the continental land mass. A biological community evolved based on intricate interrelations of soil, microorganisms, climate, and plant and animal life.

Eventually, a dynamic stasis was reached. The prairie had stabilized as the "climax" life system of the plains, perfectly balanced, adjusted to drought, extreme heat, deadly cold, strong winds, and occasional fire. The grasses were its dominant plants, tapering from tall species on the moister eastern expanses to short grasses in the dry west closer to the Rocky Mountains.

By the time scientists began studying the prairie and attempting to educate the public as to its value, it was almost too late. Successive waves of settlement, the moldboard plow, and the barbed wire fence that ended the open range and confined livestock to grazing in restricted areas had altered the ancient prairie forever. Particular species of grasses, forbs (nonwoody flowers), and legumes (the pea family) are the hallmark of undisturbed prairie. They die out when grazed too low or too frequently and, like other plants, when the soil's fertility is depleted. In the 1930s, denuded of its native plant life by overgrazing and intensive cultivation and scorched by drought, vast areas of the prairie became the Great Dust Bowl.

The miniscule bits of prairie that remain are mostly the legacy of farm families who appreciated their conservation value, productivity, and rich forage and kept them as haymeadow. This is true in Texas, as elsewhere. Even the family haymeadows in Texas continue to disappear. In 1970, Brown Collins, a graduate student at Texas A&M University working with Dr. Fred Smeins, identified seventy-five Texas "island" Blackland Prairies, ranging in size from 2 acres to several hundred. When a later student, David Diamond, conducted a second survey in 1980, only twenty-five prairies remained. The total area had shrunk from 5,000 acres—a mere scrap of its original expanse—to less than 2,000 acres.

Why should anyone care? A visit to any of the remnant prairies in Texas will show you. There is a special mystique to undisturbed prairies that inheres in even the smallest patch. The tallest of the Blackland tall grasses, Indiangrass, big bluestem, and eastern gamagrass, tower overhead in good autumns. The seedheads of little bluestem, the species that predominates in drier Texas Black-land elevations, brush a rider's stirrups in a typical fall; in moister sites it is as tall as big bluestem in autumn. The intermingled prairie plants provide an array of wildflowers in early spring, continued bloom as the grass rises in summer, and fall flowers mixed with tall, waving grasses that turn pink and gold with the advent of fall.

Iowa-born prairie writer John Madson talks about the "shaggy, fierce" quality of native prairie, "crouched" on the hills in the midst of tame, cultivated land. He talks about its quality of "surprise." In a native prairie, you know by the very look of it that you may come across things unexpected, unusual, and alive with their own beauty—native prairie is to cropland what the African veldt is to a zoo. The prairie is full of variety. In a single area, there may be scores of different species. Month by month the vista changes.

Prairie in climax condition has none of the jumbled, ragged look of land such as one sees on abandoned farms or bulldozed hillsides that people have torn up and then let go wild. The various species tend to grow in colonies according to the drainage and soil composition. One area blends into the next in subtle patterns of color and texture. There is harmonious interplay among hundreds of species of plants, insects, birds, and mammals. There is the elusive quality of wilderness—the one thing in an industrialized society that money can't buy and imported exotica can't simulate.

Steps have been taken to preserve the "wilderness park" of native Texas prairie, by the Texas Nature Conservancy, Texas Garden Clubs, Inc., the state Land Office, and numerous individuals. Small native prairies known only to their owners may exist in the Blackland and Grand Prairies. A principal concern of prairie researchers and preservationists is that knowledge of native prairie reach owners of remaining prairie land, so that they will not destroy it without realizing and appreciating its agricultural, scientific, and cultural value, to their own families and to Texas and the nation as a whole.

Tridens Prairie west of Paris, Texas, is a 97-acre remnant of one of the nation's famous haymeadows. The Texas Nature Conservancy arranged its purchase, paid for by countless small donations to the Garden Clubs of Texas in honor of the American Bicentennial. The Conservancy, with volunteer help, manages it as a public trust.

Just north of Dallas in McKinney is the newest Texas prairie project—not a virgin prairie, not a reconstructed prairie, but a transplant from Pioneer Prairie in Mesquite. Brought to public at-

Prairie dropseed (*Sporobolus silveanus*) ripples in the autumn wind on Tridens Prairie. Biologist Dave Montgomery of Paris Junior College looks over the prairie, helping the Texas Nature Conservancy maintain it for the public.

tention by Dallasite Bobby Scott in 1981, the relict prairie once owned by the Oates family became the subject of negotiations among environmentalists and developers who had recently bought it. Failing to come up with the $8 million price quoted by developers, the ad hoc group of environmentalists gave up its battle. But Ken Steigman, staff naturalist at the Heard Natural Science Museum, and his friend Jerry Saunders, an EPA enforcement official, decided late one night that if the prairie couldn't be bought, they would move it. With fifteen other hardy volunteers, they put in two or three sessions a week from November 1983 to April 1984, cutting and moving foot-square sections of sod from Pioneer Prairie in Mesquite to the Heard Sanctuary in McKinney before the bulldozers could get it. In spring, they were delighted to find the transplanted prairie, which had been watered regularly, growing taller and greener than the original. The transplant team sampled both donor and thriving transplant prairies for comparison purposes in the summer of 1984 and prepared for continued transplants in the winter of 1984–1985. Prairie chickens will be the next ingredient added, say Steigman and Saunders. Interestingly, the Pioneer Prairie remains more or less intact at this writing, the planned development having been put on hold.

East of Dallas, two quality native prairies continue under family ownership, the Lawrence Prairie owned by septuagenarian Mary Lawrence, and the Marshall family prairie in Rockwall, which is still managed as a haymeadow. The Lawrence Prairie is expected to pass eventually to Mrs. Lawrence's heirs, whose plans for the tract are unannounced. The Marshall family expresses intentions to keep their haymeadow in the family and continues to welcome prairie researchers for visits.

A prime Blackland Prairie is scheduled to be available to the public in 1986, Penn Prairie near Cedar Hill. Located in an area of the new Lakeview Park (where the Joe Pool Lake is under construction), it will be the first state Blackland Prairie park, a noteworthy accomplishment. The prairie was first brought to public attention by Parks and Wildlife ecologists on field surveys preparatory to development of the park. The prairie will be bounded by a trail with interpretive signs and made available for educational and research visits, but foot or vehicular traffic will be restricted. Prior to inclusion in the park, the prairie had been in the unbroken possession of the Penn family of Cedar Hill since the land was first surveyed. The total native prairie area amounts to 60 acres. As of 1984, about 55 acres of it were in prime climax condition, the lushest, tallest grasses and forbs that one could imagine, devoid of invader plants, thick with songbirds, quail, and grasshoppers.

Southward, between Temple and Waco, former Parks and Wildlife commissioner Bob Burleson and his wife Mickey manage 150 acres of reconstructed Blackland Prairie on their own land and a Grand Prairie ecosystem on the land of Burleson's uncle. They reconstructed these prairies using seed gathered locally and purchased, planted in worn-out farmland. "We found that by hard work and study we can plant and grow acceptable 'prairies' that we hope eventually will develop again into the climax grasslands that so amazed the early travelers through these regions of Texas," they write. Their methods and findings are available by mail in their article "Home Grown Prairies."

Another reconstructed prairie is managed by Brooks Bradley of

Alvarado, who is always ready to discuss prairie and its relation to current agricultural practices and human history, as well as his own experience managing prairie. Brooks removed 50 acres of the family ranch from production several years ago to devote to native grasses, in hopes that he would improve productivity and find relief from the escalating credit spiral of bank loans to continue capital-intensive farming practices. The subsequent success of his prairie experiment has made him a true believer.

Mildred Mauldin of Robinson, near Waco, is considered a leading expert on prairie wildflowers, with fifty years' experience in botany, ecology, seed germination, taxonomy, field studies—"everything above cell level." She and husband R. C. pioneered USDA's 1930s work with natives. They've operated Southwestern Seed Service Laboratory since 1946, testing seeds. They harvest their own for projects like their backyard Indiangrass meadow.

Dr. Geoffrey Stanford oversees native little bluestem prairie on the 1000-acre public preserve he manages in southwest Dallas County. When the land was allowed to lie fallow after the ranching operation there ended, some areas reverted to native grasses, forming large, handsome clumps of mature grasses. This sparked Stanford's interest in prairie, and led to the establishment of an experimental garden of grasses that frequently reach 7 or 8 feet in height. Stanford also designs plans for prairie gardens, one of which is included in this book. The Native Prairies Association of Texas, co-founded in 1983 by Dr. Stanford and Madge Gatlin, a Sierra Club officer, links prairie enthusiasts, the scientific community, and the public, pooling information on newly identified prairie, management techniques, and other related topics through a periodic newsletter.

The leading expert in native Texas prairie living today is E. J. Dyksterhuis, retired in Bryan after a lifetime of range management with the Soil Conservation Service and Texas A&M University. He established and continues to tend the Brazos County Arboretum's Graminetum, a display garden of native grasses.

Dr. David Riskind of the Texas Parks and Wildlife Department combines background and experience in prairie management, restoration, and ecology gained from studies and practical experience on grasslands throughout the state.

Arnold Davis of Fort Worth is another respected plantsman continuing to work on behalf of native prairie after retirement. He headed the SCS's new plant materials program for an area spanning twelve southeastern states and the Caribbean. Davis now consults; his specialty is restoring prairie by reseeding.

Even with these dedicated prairie advocates, it's difficult to de-

Big bluestem, "turkey foot" to the pioneers and "man's beard" or *Andropogon* to botanists, is dubbed "prince of the prairie" for its high protein content and wide geographic range.

Julie Ryan

Julie Ryan

Delicate little bluestem glows in afternoon sunlight on the prairie at Greenhills Environmental Center in Dallas.

Julie Ryan

Eastern gamagrass (*Tripsacum dactyloides*) dates back three or four million years to the late Tertiary. Its relative *Zea mays* was bred by American Indians to develop corn.

Heard Natural Science Museum

Indiangrass blooms in fall, reaching up to 8 feet in height.

201

Sideoats grama, the state grass of Texas, remains attractive even in winter with its pendants of seed and provides essential forage on Texas ranges.

Benny J. Simpson

velop a plan for preserving prairie without an accurate inventory and evaluation of the prairies that remain. After decades of survey work by isolated individuals, a complete survey of Texas tall-grass prairie was scheduled for 1984 release. This prairie survey is the first published study of the Natural Heritage Program of the state's General Land Office, established in 1984 to survey remaining natural areas of Texas. Early new "finds" include ten prairies over 300 acres.

The remaining prairie offers more than history, conservation, and beauty. It is the last of the rich, living factory of soil, plant, and animal life that was the basis of American agriculture. Americans could not resist overdrawing on the rich storehouse of soil that developed in the Central Plains over 25 million years. It was the credit in nature's account that funded our emergence as a nation and the "breadbasket" of the world. The problem is that the wilderness is now subdued, and the soil bank is nearing bankruptcy, kept productive only by massive infusions of chemical fertilizers, herbicides, and pesticides. The undisturbed prairie is the last preserve of the land in its original balance, a laboratory to show us whether nature has answers we missed in our previous subjugation of the land, first by European farming methods and then by chemical-based technologies and imported plant species.

What can the prairie teach us? What can it add to our standardized town and city landscapes? Unless the trend is reversed, homemade prairies may be all that remains to remind us of a prairie heritage lost forever.

A prairie to copy from nature could brighten a southwestern lawn, with a gentle slope of mid-grasses, Drummond's phlox, white prickly poppy, and bluebonnets, shaded by a mesquite tree.

10

Prairie Everywhere

WHAT can you do with a prairie? Besides lounge in it, chewing an Indiangrass straw—watching the butterflies play and relishing the sunwarmed hay against your back? Isn't that enough?

Beryl Nolen of Fort Worth has inherited a "pocket prairie" that other people could achieve with a little effort. In the Glengarden addition where she lives, residential subdivisions were set down in the middle of native tall-grass prairie. Vestiges of it remain on the limestone bluffs overlooking Cobb Park. On lower elevations terraced with home sites, prairie still breaks through. On Glengarden Drive, wildflowers and short prairie grass bloom throughout the growing season, in an array of thirty or more wildflowers, including verbena, thelesperma, and cut-leaf daisy.

Marcia and Cecil Coale of McKinney have planted the land adjoining their front drive with native bluestem. Visitors approach their contemporary home through an expanse of silvery prairie that subsides to turf grass and gardens. Marcia provides information on native prairie and gardens through her Wildflower Hotline (see Sources).

Ken Steigman of Plano grows a buffalo grass lawn mowed to a height even with his neighbor's Bermuda turf. They appear identical, except for the buffalo grass's blue-green tint—and the absence of lawn sprinklers, except in the hottest months. Allowed to grow to its full 3- or 4-inch height, buffalo grass has a translucent, feathery look, and it flowers with tiny orange or purple blooms that become white fringes of seed.

In the largest urban spaces—airports, the edges of ballparks, and parklands—the prairie could be re-created. This would take work to establish, but after the start-up period, the replica prairie should almost take care of itself, as native American prairies did for millions of years. Mowing or controlled burns could control scrub growth, as wildfire and grazing buffalo once did. Short-grass species could be selected for areas where tall growth is undesirable; and both cool-season and warm-season native grasses are available to provide a long season of greenery. The irreplaceable native prairie that was aeons in the making can't be duplicated by human beings in a few years. We can, in a short time, copy its most delightful features for our landscapes, however. Native prairie is like an old-fashioned bouquet, a medley of flowers and grasses, of patterns, colors, and scents, that you can look at again and again and discover still more to enjoy. It changes with each season. It changes from year to year, as nature perfects the gardener's design, each perennial species seeking its ideally suited spot in the terrain.

In areas of several acres or more, one can reconstruct a prairie as similar as possible to the prairie that originally existed on the land. "A "replica" or reconstructed prairie can serve as a personal nature preserve—possibly even meet a rancher's practical need for better haymeadow.

A "pocket prairie" fits the dimensions of home landscapes or vacant lots. Its small area can sustain a wide variety of the plants of the original prairie. It doesn't have to imitate slavishly every detail of the original prairie of its locale. For instance, a mid-grass like blue grama or a short grass like buffalo grass could be substituted in areas that historically grew tall grasses, in order to satisfy municipal ordinances on grass height. A pocket prairie is far more varied than a conventional lawn or groundcover landscape, and, once established, it takes less maintenance.

With a prairie garden, one can impose a more definite design, a more controlled look. Like an old-fashioned garden, a prairie garden is a mixture of many intermingled plants, but with the striking addition of grasses. One can leave behind the discipline of weeded beds, and let the prairie flowers and grasses grow thickly together, defining the garden with rock borders or flagstone paths.

Another use of prairie in landscapes is simply to select one or more varieties for inclusion in a conventional garden, such as sideoats grama in a border or Maximilian daisy against a wall. Many of the plants featured in this book are plants of the climax prairie. As isolated plants in a traditional flower bed, they are hardy and adapted to local conditions, as long as you keep their abstemious habits in mind and don't over-water or over-fertilize them. This may be the only agreeable prairie application for formal tastes.

To my mind, the most original and visually interesting of these landscape options would be plantings in true prairie style. They offer the variety and surprise of prairie as prairie. A well-defined pocket prairie area could enliven a conventional turf grass and shrub landscape. A prairie garden could bring a more sculpted design of seasonal flowers and grasses in leaf, flower, and seed to your window. Depending on the setting, either one would appear uniquely contemporary in its freedom of form or very rustic, reminiscent of pioneer days.

But first one must face facts. A can of prepackaged prairie seeds opened and tossed onto bare ground will not produce what can properly be called prairie. It may not even sprout. Prairie takes some effort to start, as does any landscape. The seeds or seedlings have to be selected not only for your region, but for your particular site. But when the planning and preparation are done correctly, and the plants are well established, then the benefits of minimal maintenance and low water requirements pay off generously.

Prairie plants are adapted to full sun. Some have success in shade, but well-shaded sites are not recommended for plantings using the grasses featured in this book. If you really would like to have prairie in your shady landscape, plan it as a small area in a sunny spot.

Seedlings and seeds from your region are best. Why try to grow an Iowa prairie in Texas? Even if an out-of-state seed supplier has a particular species that also grows in Texas, it is not likely to be as well adapted to growing conditions here as local seed. Locally harvested seed is best, gathered sparingly. Or try local farm and ranch dealers, nurseries, and suppliers suggested by the Soil Conservation Service in your area. If seed for a plant you would particularly like to have is not available, then consider out-of-state sources. Seed houses in the Midwest and West offer prairie seeds. The more accurately you select the species for your site, the more readily the plants will maintain your original design through successive seasons. This means paying attention to the soil composition and planting accordingly. Moisture levels are important, too; plant moisture-loving grasses in the low spots and dry-land plants in higher elevations. Consult Gould's *Grasses of Texas* for ones naturally occurring in your region. It is a good idea to include both fall-blooming, warm-season grasses and spring-blooming, cool-season grasses. This provides two bloom seasons and almost

Julie Ryan

Glengarden Drive in Fort Worth inherited this "pocket prairie" of wild verbena and thelesperma.

year-round greenery. You can allow the attractive seed heads to stand on the dormant grasses or clip them. Composting and inter-planting with legumes improve plant growth in soils that aren't as rich as the original prairie.

Consider the amount of maintenance you're willing to devote as you plan your prairie landscape. Prairie plantings may take some defending against aggressive introduced species like Johnson grass and against regrowth of plants originally on the site. Small prairie areas the size of a city lot or less take as much help fighting weeds as conventional lawns or gardens until they take root firmly and spread. Resist the temptation to use wholesale applications of herbicide to prepare the site; people working with prairie land-scapes instead recommend thorough tilling and subsequent timed mowings to wipe out weeds gradually. Some suggest careful spot

Buffalo grass blankets a suburban lawn, grown to full 4-inch height and speckled with delicate seed heads.

applications of biodegradable herbicides. A prairie planting with grasses, forbs, and legumes, intermingled and allowed to grow as thick as they will, capitalizes on the original prairie's weed-resistant, drought-resistant, soil-enriching qualities. It gradually develops a thick sod that resists invasion by other plants. The immense leaf surface area and the sod absorb rainfall. Winter growth, cut and let fall, forms a mulch that eventually decomposes to rich humus. This, together with the nitrogen-fixing action of legumes and the activity of soil microbes, makes the prairie self-fertilizing. You don't need to use commercial fertilizers; they encourage weeds and don't help native grasses, say experts. The sod and mulch also inhibit weed growth; when you use prairie plants in a conventional weeded flower bed with space around each plant, you lose the prairie's native weed-resisting ability. In general, it's

209

Benny J. Simpson

Feathery seed tops of Lindheimer's muhly (*Muhlenbergia lindheimeri*) rival Argentine pampas grass as a showy landscape plant.

probable that the more you depart from the design of the original prairie in your created landscape, the more of its special benefits you will lose. But even when used in formal plantings radically different from their natural habitat, prairie flowers, feathery tall-grass clumps, and short-grass borders and lawns offer attractiveness and hardiness to equal that of our accustomed garden plants, a new array from which to choose.

In this chapter you will find Dr. Geoffrey Stanford's directions for making a "pocket prairie" and a garden plan by him and Sally Wasowski, with lists of the plants included. In addition, Bob and Mickey Burleson of Temple have provided an excerpt from their report "Home Grown Prairies" giving recommendations based on experience reconstructing prairies. For information on specific plants, refer to the index of this book and the Bibliography and Sources.

Prairie gardening is a far cry from selecting plants at the local nursery and installing them according to a detailed plan from a garden magazine. The plants available are not even widely known. Visits to prairie preserves are a good starting point, with an identification guide to help. Aspiring prairie gardeners should get to know their own land, if they don't already, by observing soil characteristics and the existing vegetation. Prairie preservationists and ecologists, contacted through private and governmental organizations, are most helpful in the education process. Currently the Soil Conservation Service, Greenhills Center, and Texas Agricultural Extension Service consult with private landowners, and the Texas Department of Parks and Wildlife is available for consultation on public lands, regarding prairie and prairie maintenance. There has yet to be a book about prairie gardening in Texas, but works from other regions are applicable, for general principles.

The original prairie pioneers struck out into the unknown. Perhaps now people can strike out to rediscover the unknown, amid our all-too-predictable standardized environments, and bring the mystery and awe of the prairie home to us.

PRAIRIE GARDEN

This plan is inspired by a design done by Dr. Geoffrey Stanford of Greenhills. It uses prairie grasses and flowers chosen to give year-round interest and color. The flowers are mostly yellow and pink, providing spots of color from spring to frost. The grasses get feathery flowers and seed heads that are quite showy. The seed head of Indiangrass is a beautiful bright gold. In the fall, the stems and leaves turn golden, silver, or pinkish.

The garden as a whole is quite short in February, when the new green shoots start pushing up. As the season progresses, the stems of some of these plants will get over 9 feet tall. The table gives the heights and bloom times of the plants used. You might notice that some of the heights given are taller than for the same plant in the body of the book. This is because the flowers tend to grow taller when they are mixed with grasses. They have to extend themselves to compete for the sun, and the grasses help support their stems. Whether or not specimens reach the maximum heights depends on the richness of your soil and the amount of water they get. It will take two or three years for your garden to get established and stable. At first, species like the Maximilian daisy may grow abnormally tall. Then, as the other species take hold, they will compete for moisture and nutrients and limit each other's growth. David Riskind of Texas Parks and Wildlife recommends dense plantings to encourage the natural competition.

This prairie garden is designed to go in a lawn or a patio in full sun. The narrowest point is almost 20 feet wide, so that the 9-foot plants will not be overwhelming. If you do not have space for a bed this large, eliminate the tallest plants. To give you a wide variety of prairie in a very small space, the center of this garden has been excavated 3 inches to form a swale to make an area for moisture-loving flowers and grasses. The soil from this excavation is piled up on the edges 3 inches high to form an area for plants that like to be well drained at all times. Make the larger area of elevation at the lower end of your garden, so it can catch and hold water efficiently, using the natural drainage of your lawn or patio. Water the swale by putting the garden hose into the depression and letting it run until the area is flooded. Repeat when dried out, every two to three weeks. In addition, all the plantings will need periodic waterings. The first year, water once a week. In successive years, how much you water will depend on your soil, the weather, and how green you want your garden to look. If the vine-mesquite starts becoming a nuisance, you are watering too much. If you want a more drought-tolerant prairie garden, eliminate the swale, but give supplemental deep waterings for two years before letting it be on its own, and always water in a drought or expect to lose some plants.

The plants in the swale and on ground level are typical of a climax tall-grass prairie. The buffalo grass, sideoats grama, and purple paintbrush on the raised level are found in short-grass prairie and in burned or otherwise disturbed areas of tall-grass prairie.

The buffalo grass provides a gentle transition from the lawn or patio to the height of the little bluestem, so that you are not viewing an abrupt wall of grass. The mortared brick edging is designed to separate the grasses in your prairie garden from your mown lawn, both visually and to reduce weeding. For the first couple of years while the perennials are maturing, plan to spend quite a lot of time rooting out undesirable specimens. Once your garden has grown dense, you will probably have to weed only in the spring to get out unwanted seedlings and sprouted trees. Every February, cut the dead stalks no lower than 4 inches to prepare for the new season's growth.

Prairie Garden		
Common Name/Latin Name	Height	Bloom Time
SWALE		
Eastern Gamagrass *Tripsacum dactyloides*	5–10 feet	Summer–Fall
Vine-Mesquite *Panicum obtusum*	8–32 inches	Spring–Fall
Switchgrass *Panicum virgatum*	3–6 (9) feet	Late summer–Fall
Lionheart (Fall) *Physostegia praemorsa*	3–4 feet	August–October
Maximilian Daisy *Helianthus maximiliani*	2–10 feet	September–October

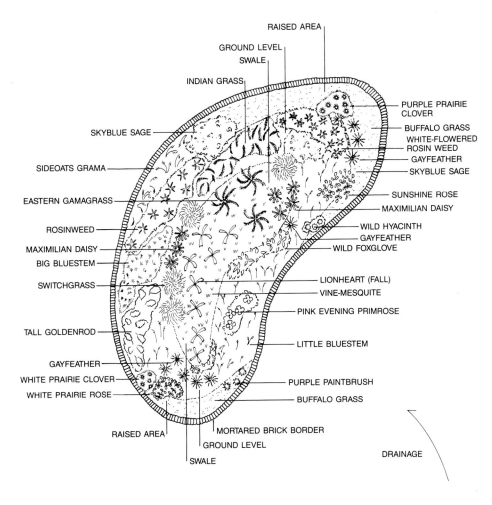

RAISED AREA
GROUND LEVEL
SWALE
INDIAN GRASS
SKYBLUE SAGE
SIDEOATS GRAMA
EASTERN GAMAGRASS
ROSINWEED
MAXIMILIAN DAISY
BIG BLUESTEM
SWITCHGRASS
TALL GOLDENROD
GAYFEATHER
WHITE PRAIRIE CLOVER
WHITE PRAIRIE ROSE
RAISED AREA
MORTARED BRICK BORDER
GROUND LEVEL
SWALE

PURPLE PRAIRIE CLOVER
BUFFALO GRASS
WHITE-FLOWERED ROSIN WEED
GAYFEATHER
SKYBLUE SAGE
SUNSHINE ROSE
MAXIMILIAN DAISY
WILD HYACINTH
GAYFEATHER
WILD FOXGLOVE
LIONHEART (FALL)
VINE-MESQUITE
PINK EVENING PRIMROSE
LITTLE BLUESTEM
PURPLE PAINTBRUSH
BUFFALO GRASS
DRAINAGE

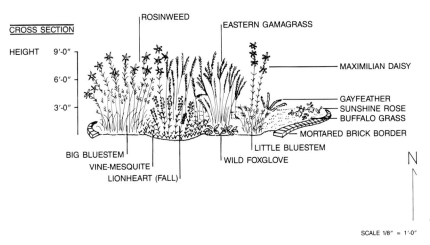

CROSS SECTION

HEIGHT
9'-0"
6'-0"
3'-0"

ROSINWEED
EASTERN GAMAGRASS
MAXIMILIAN DAISY
GAYFEATHER
SUNSHINE ROSE
BUFFALO GRASS
MORTARED BRICK BORDER
BIG BLUESTEM
VINE-MESQUITE
LIONHEART (FALL)
WILD FOXGLOVE
LITTLE BLUESTEM

N

SCALE 1/8" = 1'-0"

Prairie Garden

GROUND LEVEL

Indiangrass *Sorghastrum nutans*	3–8 feet	Late summer–Fall
Big Bluestem *Andropogon gerardi*	3–6 feet	Late summer–Fall
Little Bluestem *Andropogon scoparius*	1–3 (5) feet	Summer–Fall
Rosinweed *Silphium asperrimum*	5–8 feet	Summer
White-Flowered Rosinweed *Silphium albiflorum*	2–3 feet	Summer
Wild Foxglove *Penstemon cobaea*	2 feet	April–May
Tall Goldenrod *Solidago altissima*	3–7 feet	October
Pink Evening Primrose *Oenothera speciosa*	1–2 feet	April–June

RAISED AREA

Buffalo Grass *Buchloe dactyloides*	3–6 inches	Spring–Summer–Fall
Sideoats Grama *Bouteloua curtipendula*	2–3 feet	Late spring–Fall
Sunshine Rose *Rosa suffulta*	1–2 feet	May–August
White Prairie Rose *Rosa foliolosa*	1–2 feet	April–June
Skyblue Sage *Salvia azurea*	3–5 feet	July–October
Purple Prairie Clover *Petalostemum pulcherrimum* (often misidentified as *P. purpureum*)	1–2 feet	May–July
White Prairie Clover *Petalostemum multiflorum*	1–2 feet	June–July
Purple Paintbrush *Castilleja purpurea* (variety for your area)	1 foot	April–May
Wild Hyacinth *Camassia scilloides*	1–2 feet	March–May

BUFFALO GRASS LAWN

Buffalo grass is our only native turf grass. That means that it takes more heat and drought and cold than St. Augustine, zoysia, and even Bermuda. It grows naturally only 4–5 inches tall, so mowing it is optional. Unmown, it looks like a sea of soft, blue-

Buffalo grass (*Buchloe dactyloides*) speckled with delicate seed heads.

green waves. If you don't water it, it will turn a soft golden brown in the summer. By going dormant like this, it is conserving water. It will turn green in the fall, then go dormant again in the winter to protect itself from the cold, and turn green in the spring when it blossoms. There are male and female plants. The female's blossoms are close to the earth where the seed won't get grazed. The male's blossoms are more conspicuous and range in color from coral to red. The seed is inside a hard coat called a "burr," which makes germination a slow process. For this reason, it is desirable to buy specially treated seed. Some is treated to speed up germination, and some is treated with a fungicide to keep the seed disease-free while it germinates. It requires a soil temperature of 70° F for germination, so planting time in North Texas is from approximately April 15 to September 1 (it may be both earlier and later in warmer parts of the state). Till the seed bed no deeper than 2 inches, but enough to cover the seed. After broadcasting the seed, tamp or roll the seed bed firmly so that a hard rain cannot wash the seed down too far to germinate.

The seed is very heavy, so if you buy a pound of buffalo grass seed, you are getting only about 50,000 seeds, whereas you would get 1,500,000 in a pound of Bermuda grass seed. It is also expensive, because so little is being produced at this time. This means that you have to be very rich or sow it more thinly. At the rate of 3–4 pounds per 1,000 square feet, it will take two to three years to get a dense lawn. Applying a 3-1-2 fertilizer at the rate of 7 pounds per 1,000 square feet in early May can speed up the process. A little judicious watering can also help. If you water in the summer every time the grass blades start to turn brown, you can prevent it from going dormant, thereby extending its growth period. It will send out stolons, like Bermuda grass, which will root and gradually fill in all the sparsely covered areas. Don't water or fertilize it more than this, or you will give the weeds and unwanted grasses an unfair advantage. Buffalo grass is adapted to 12–25 inches of rain annually for optimum growth. Under these conditions it is almost immune to pests and diseases. Enjoy the freedom it can give you. If you do want to mow it, never cut it shorter than 2 inches. Mown and watered in the summer, it looks pretty much like a normal turf grass. It does have one limitation; it will not tolerate any shade at all. There wasn't a lot of shade on the prairie, so this is an adaption it didn't make.

HOW TO START A POCKET PRAIRIE

I'm a little prairie flower
Growing wilder ev'ry hour
Nobody cares to cultivate me
'Cause I'm as wild as wild can be
George Formby, English music-hall song

What if you do care? How do you set about it? Is there a minimum size? Are prairie grasses and flowers different from any others? In what ways? Can you really grow grasses 9 feet tall? Will the Fire Department tell you to mow them down to 12 inches?

Let's take the last question first. No, they won't. They don't tell you to mow down your pampas grass or your rambling rose. If you keep your yard neat, and you have a bed of tall-growing plants in it, they will recognize it as such even if they don't recognize the plants.

Our true prairie tall grasses, and their accompanying colorful flowers, have one special characteristic: they store a lot of water and energy in their roots before winter starts, so they can grow fast in spring even if there is too little rainfall. Those roots go

Prairie flowers grace the plains in a vivid mixture of thelesperma, yellow evening primrose, pink sensitive briar (*Schrankia*), bluebonnets, and winecups.

down many feet, so they can get water even during a long summer drought. These plants are all perennials: some grass clumps can live at least 20 years, and some flowers maybe even longer.

In the early spring, the prairie is carpeted with short-stemmed flowers: ten-petal anemone, white camas, celestial, perennial purple Indian paintbrush. As these start to set seed, the tall grasses start to grow their spring leaves: big and little bluestems, Indiangrass, switchgrass, eastern gamagrass. In a year of good rainfall some leaves will reach 3 to 4 feet and more by the end of June: their true length is masked by their graceful arching fall.

Under their cover of the grasses, the spikes of the second wave of flowers grow up: the two tall species of yellow compass-plant, skyblue sage, Maximilian daisy, Engelmann daisy, goldenrod. By the end of June, the leaves of the grasses are fully mature, and the flowering spikes, called "culms," start to grow. As they reach and then overtop their leaves, the flowers elongate, always keeping a little above them; but since the grasses grow thickly, and the flowers are dotted here and there, they do not compete for sunlight with the grasses. By late fall, all have set seed, and then the culms turn purple-brown and stay so till next spring—gorgeous in winter sunset, splendid when snow-spattered.

You can grow your prairie grasses from seed, if you know what you are looking for, and harvest them yourself by hand. Put each species in a labeled paper sack, and store them at room temperature for a month or two. In late February, mix four volumes of the mix with one volume of finely powdered chalk; put small pinches of this mix into your soil 18 inches apart and cover each with half an inch of soil. Do this for each species separately. You can interplant each species in the soil, pinch by pinch—but do not mix them all together in a single bag. Now (this is very important) tread them down hard. After planting, water them thoroughly once every week if it does not rain, right through until the end of July.

Under this regime a lot of weeds may come in because of your irrigation. Whenever those get to 12 inches high, mow them back to 4 inches (but no lower, or you will mow off your young prairie growth). In addition, mow two or three times in the first year to control weeds. Continue to mow the entire area annually during the first week of February to cut down the trash and let sunlight onto the early spring growth. The first year you may have to mow three or four times in all; the second year you may have to mow two or three times; and from then on, the early February mowing should be adequate to control weeds.

Planting flower seeds is different: follow planting instructions for each species. You will probably find it difficult to collect your own seed; since these plants are rare, you may have to buy them. You will do best to plant them in the fall of the year in which you planted the grass seed—that is, some seven to eight months later. They will take two or three years to come to flowering size, but why should a 70,000-year-old prairie flower be in a hurry?

But if you are in a hurry, you may prefer to buy and plant roots in September, of both grasses and flowers, and get a fine display the very next year, if there is a supplier in your area.

These plants have different soil moisture requirements, so our garden plan advises that you prepare the soil by digging out the center of your patch about 4 inches deep and stack the earth you have removed round the edge to make a slightly raised border. Plant the moisture lovers in the central depression, and the dryland lovers on the tops of the raised edges. We list the species in order of moisture requirement. All of them prefer irrigation during their first year, whether growing from seed or from root; but you can rely on natural rainfall (or drought) every year thereafter for all but the wet-land lovers. For those you should flood the center of your depressed patch once every two or three weeks during the hot summer (but not every week).

One further point: you may have noticed that I have not mentioned any of those gorgeous Texas spring wildflowers: bluebonnet, firewheel, red Indian paintbrush, golden wave. These are all annuals; they appear in disturbed or over-grazed areas in tallgrass prairie.

Of course, the real native prairie has many more plants than these; but once you have got these growing well for you, you will want to read about more—and more, and more. And to plant those, too. Beware! Getting hooked on prairie plants is a creeping disease, but with a difference: as it progresses you get healthier and happier. Have fun!

—Dr. Geoffrey Stanford
Greenhills Environmental Center

WHAT IT TAKES TO START A REPLICA PRAIRIE

In general, we feel that the following are essential items in starting a replica prairie . . .

. . . land, preferably 5 acres or more, that can be permanently devoted to this use. We started with a farm of 100 acres, about 40 acres of which was "worn-out" land no longer suitable for row crops. We devoted this worn-out land to the prairie project, and later expanded into the better land as we could afford to take it out of row crop production. Prairies can be created on smaller plots, but it is better to have several acres so that you can get a full plant and animal community going, strong enough to resist invading weeds and grasses from outside.

. . . time to collect seeds, mainly by hand at first, from roadsides and native prairie remnants in your area. We worked nearly every weekend for a year to collect the several hundred pounds of native forb, legume, and grass seeds that we used in our first plantings, and it was nearly all collected by hand.

. . . a small tractor or shredder, or access to one, to mow and control competitive weed growth during the first two years of the project. It is not essential in all cases to mow to cut down the competition, but it speeds the establishment of a good stand better than anything else, and when you work that hard for seed, you don't want to waste any of it in competition with weeds.

. . . rain and good luck. Almost everything else can be improvised, rented, or borrowed.

The true cost of anything is the amount of your time that you must exchange in order to obtain it. Prairies don't cost a lot of cash, but they are expensive in respect to time, and there is no

Julie Ryan

Pioneer Prairie in July mixes Indiangrass and prairie mimosa with the seed pods of spring-blooming coneflower and purple prairie clover, plants that can be used in creating a "replica" prairie.

point in getting involved with them unless you are willing to see it through to the end. It takes at least two years to see your labors really bear fruit when you are dealing with native grasses and forbs.

You will not know what to collect at first and will not know what you are looking at. So in the beginning you will be wandering around in remnant prairies just looking, starting with the first growth of plants in the spring, and seeing what comes up, what it looks like at first, what it develops into, and when and how it flowers and bears fruit. If you read widely in the literature that is available on prairies, you will educate yourself as you go, and soon will know which plants "belong" and which do not. By spending successive weekends in prairie plots, you will soon get a feel for the total plant community in the prairie, and then, as you see members of this community blooming on roadsides and in waste places, you can add to your inventory of seed source. No degree in botany is required, and with the many books that are available to help you in your first efforts at plant identification, any intelligent person can become a pretty fair lay botanist with respect to the native prairie plants of his or her area.

—Bob and Mickey Burleson

Bibliography

Abbott, Carroll. *How to Know and Grow Texas Wildflowers.* Green Horizons Press, 500 Thompson Drive, Kerrville, Texas 78028, 1979.

Ajilvsgi, Geyata. *Wildflowers of the Big Thicket, East Texas and Western Louisiana.* Texas A&M University Press, College Station and London, 1979.

————. *Wildflowers of Texas.* Shearer Publishing, Bryan, Texas, 1984.

Albrecht, W. A. *The Albrecht Papers.* Acres U.S.A., Kansas City, Missouri 64133.

Archer, Sellers G. and Clarence E. Bunch. *The American Grass Book.* University of Oklahoma Press, Norman, 1953.

Betz, Robert F. "The Vanishing Prairie: Its Glory Once Was an Ecologist's Dream." *Science.* April, 1980.

Bradley, Brooks. "Why the Climax Natives?" Unpublished essay.

Burleson, Bob and Mickey Burleson. "Home Grown Prairies." Bob and Mickey Burleson, Box 844, Temple, Texas 76501. (Unpublished; write them for a copy.)

Correll, D. S. and M. C. Johnston. *Manual of the Vascular Plants of Texas.* Contributions from Texas Research Foundation, A Series of Botanical Studies edited by Cyrus Longworth Lundell, Vol. 6, University of Texas at Dallas, 1979.

Directory to Resources on Wildflower Propagation. National Council of State Garden Clubs, Inc., 1981, pp. 88–123.

Duffield, Mary Rose and Warren D. Jones. *Plants for Dry Climates.* H. P. Books, Tucson, Arizona, 1981.

Duncan, Patricia D. "Forgotten Treasure: Our Tall-Grass Prairie." *Modern Maturity.* June–July, 1979.

Dyas, Robert W. "The Flora of Tridens Prairie." Slide presentation, Texas Nature Conservancy, 1981.

Dyksterhuis, E. J. "The Vegetation of the Fort Worth Prairie." *Ecological Monographs.* Volume 16, No. 1, January, 1946.

Edwards, Tom. "Buffalo and Prairie Ecology." *Proceedings of Fifth Midwest Prairie Conference.* Iowa State University, Ames, Iowa, 1976.

Farney, Dennis. "The Tallgrass Prairie: Can It Be Saved?" *National Geographic.* January, 1980.

Foster, Gertrude B. and Rosemary F. Louden. *Park's Success with Herbs.* Geo. W. Park Seed Co., Inc., Greenwood, South Carolina, 1980.

Garrett, Howard. *Plants of the Metroplex.* Lantana Press, Dallas, Texas, 1975.

Geological Highway Map of Texas, U.S. Geological Highway Map Series, Map. No. 7. American Association of Petroleum Geologists, P.O. Box 979, Tulsa, Oklahoma 74101, 1973.

Gould, Frank W. *The Grasses of Texas.* Texas A&M University Press, College Station, 1975.

Kennedy, Maggie. "Prairie Preservation." *Dallas Times Herald.* May 12, 1983.

King, Madonna Luers. "Preserving the Tallgrass Prairie." *Sierra.* May–June, 1984.

Kittel, Mary Badham. *Our Vast and Varied Vacation Land.* Texas Garden Clubs, Inc., Fort Worth, Texas, 1964.

Loughmiller, Campbell and Lynn Loughmiller. *Texas Wildflowers.* University of Texas Press, Austin, Texas, 1984.

Madson, John. *Where the Sky Began*. Houghton Mifflin Company, Boston, 1982.

Reilly, Ann. *Park's Success with Seeds*. Geo. W. Park Seed Co., Inc., Greenwood, South Carolina, 1978.

Rickett, Harold William. *Wild Flowers of the United States*. Vol. 3, Parts 1 and 2. McGraw-Hill Book Co., New York, 1969.

Riskind, David H. and O. Brown Collins. "The Blackland Prairie of Texas: Conservation of Representative Climax Remnants." In *Prairie: A Multiple View*, edited by M. K. Wali. University of North Dakota Press, Grand Forks, North Dakota, 1972.

Scheider, Alfred F. *Park's Success with Bulbs*. Geo. W. Park Seed Co., Inc., Greenwood, South Carolina, 1981.

Schulz, Ellen D. *Texas Wild Flowers*. Laidlaw Brothers, Chicago and New York, 1928.

Sheldon, Robert A. *Roadside Geology of Texas*. Mountain Press Publishing Co., 279 West Front Street, Missoula, Montana 59801, 1979.

Shinners, Lloyd H. *Shinners' Spring Flora*. SMU Herbarium, Dallas, Texas 75275, 1958.

Silverstein, Stuart and David Hurlbut. "Loan Official Expected to Quit in Condo Probe." *Dallas Times Herald*. December 17, 1983.

Smeins, Fred E. "Texas Prairie: Roots of Our Culture." Presentation at the Dallas Museum of Natural History, September 15, 1983.

Smith, J. Robert. *The Prairie Garden*. University of Wisconsin Press, 1974.

"Soil Survey of Dallas County, Texas." USDA Soil Conservation Service in cooperation with Texas Agricultural Experiment Station, February, 1980.

"Special Publication of the Society for Louisiana Irises." Lafayette, Louisiana 70504, 1981.

Sperry, Neil. *Neil Sperry's Complete Guide to Texas Gardening*. Taylor Publishing Company, Dallas, Texas, 1982.

Stillwell, Norma. *Key and Guide to the Woody Plants of Dallas County*. Proctor-Adams Printing Service, Dallas, Texas, April, 1939.

Texas Wildflower Newsletter. Vols. 4:1–8:3. Green Horizons, 500 Thompson Drive, Kerrville, Texas 78028, 1979–1984.

Tobey, Ronald C. *Saving the Prairies: The Life Cycle of the Founding School of American Plant Ecology, 1895–1955*. University of California Press, Berkeley and Los Angeles, California, 1981.

Vines, Robert A. *Trees, Shrubs, and Woody Vines of the Southwest*. University of Texas Press, Austin and London, 1960.

———. *Trees of North Texas*. University of Texas Press, Austin, Texas, 1982.

Warnock, Barton H. *Wildflowers of the Big Bend Country of Texas*. Sul Ross State University, Alpine, Texas, 1970.

Weaver, J. E. and T. J. Fitzpatrick. "The Prairie." *Ecological Monographs*, Vol. 4. Duke University Press, Durham, North Carolina, 1934.

Whitehouse, Eula. *Texas Flowers in Natural Colors*. Eula Whitehouse, Dallas, Texas, 1936.

Wills, Mary Motz and Howard S. Irwin. *Roadside Flowers of Texas*. University of Texas Press, Austin, Texas, 1961.

Wyman, Donald. *Wyman's Gardening Encyclopedia*. Macmillan Publishing Co., Inc., New York, 1971.

Notes from lectures by Benny Simpson, Carroll Abbott, Barry Kridler, and Jill Nokes at various courses, seminars, and Wildflower Days.

Sources

Local

Public gardens, natural history or science museums, nature preserves, and the district offices of the USDA Soil Conservation Service are the best places to start looking for plants and seeds suitable to your particular area, because most of these organizations have newsletters and keep up-to-date lists of suppliers.

State

Native Plant Society of Texas, P.O. Box 23836, Texas Woman's University, Denton, Texas 76204.
There are chapters for North, Central, West, East, Coastal, and South Texas. Newsletters, seed exchanges, plant sales, and so forth.
Native Prairies Association of Texas, Greenhills Center, 7575 Wheatland Road, Dallas, Texas 75249.
Texas Garden Clubs, Inc., 3111 Botanic Garden Road, Fort Worth, Texas 76107.
Texas Native Plant Directory of the Texas Department of Agriculture, P.O. Box 12847, Austin, Texas 78711.
This is your most important source for nursery plants.
Wildflower Hotline, Marcia Coale, McKinney, Texas, (214) 542-1947.

National

National Wildflower Research Center, P.O. Box 1011, Austin, Texas 78767.

Computer bank of suppliers and other information.
Society for Louisiana Irises, Box 40175 U.S.L., Lafayette, Louisiana 70504.
"Sources of Native Seeds and Plants," Soil Conservation Society of America, 7515 Northeast Ankeny Road, Ankeny, Iowa 50021.

Habitat Preservation

Greenhills Environmental Center, 7575 Wheatland Road, Dallas, Texas 75249.
Heard Natural Science Museum, Route 6, Box 22, McKinney, Texas 75069.
Texas Committee on Natural Resources, 5518 Dyer, Suite 3B, Dallas, Texas 75206.
Texas Natural Heritage Program, General Land Office, Stephen F. Austin Building, 1700 Congress Avenue, Austin, Texas 78767.
Texas Nature Conservancy, 503 B East Sixth Street, Austin, Texas 78701.
Wild Basin Wilderness, P.O. Box 13455, Austin, Texas 78711.

Annual Public Events

Flora-Rama, Austin Garden Center, Zilker Park, Austin, Texas 78704.
Texas Wildflower Day, Texas Woman's University, P.O. Box 22939, Denton, Texas 76204.
Wildflower Day, Tridens Prairie, Dave Montgomery, Science Department, Paris Junior College, Paris, Texas 75460.
Wildflower Trails of Texas at Hughes Springs, P.O. Box 608, Hughes Springs, Texas 75656.

223

Wildflower Workshop, Greenhills Environmental Center, 7575 Wheatland Road, Dallas, Texas 75249.

Seeds and/or Plants by Mail

Send for a catalog to find out which plants each place supplies. You have to pay for most of these catalogs, but the cost is usually deducted from your first order.

Bob Turner Seed Company, Route 1, Box 292, Breckinridge, Texas 76024, (817) 559-2065.

Gone Native, 2001 Broken Hills Road East, Route 4, Midland, Texas 47970, (915) 686-9632.

Greenhills Environmental Center, 7575 Wheatland Road, Dallas, Texas 75249. Write or call at (214) 296-1955.

Green Horizons, 500 Thompson Drive, Kerrville, Texas 78028.

Native Plants Reclamation Services, 9180 S. Wasatch Blvd., Sandy, Utah 84092, (801) 943-3288.

Park Seed, Cokesbury Road, Greenwood, South Carolina 29647.

Plants of the Southwest, 1570 Pacheco St., Santa Fe, New Mexico 87501.

Southwestern Native Seeds, Box 50503, Tucson, Arizona 85703.

Texas Natives, 910 Glen Oak, Austin, Texas 78745.

Wayside Gardens, Hodges, South Carolina, 29695, (800) 845-1124. Plants only.

For other suppliers, contact the National Wildflower Research Center, P.O. Box 1011, Austin, Texas 78767.

Plants from Nurseries

Write for the "Texas Native Plant Directory" from the Texas Department of Agriculture, P.O. Box 12847, Austin, Texas 78711, for a current listing of nurseries all over the state that carry native plants.

Index

SALLY WASOWSKI, landscape designer, works out of her Dallas home, where she also practices the professions of wife and mother. A specialist in native plants, she uses her front yard as an experimental garden; it has been featured in *Dallas/Fort Worth Home & Garden*. Early on, Sally recognized a real need for a reference book that would detail not only specific native flowers and trees but also how to use them. Unable to find such a book, she decided to create it herself. With help from her freelance-writer husband, she wrote the sections of this book that describe the plants, how to grow them, and how to landscape with them.

JULIE RYAN has written about wilderness preservation and native plants, as well as business and historic topics, for many Texas magazines. She writes scripts for educational and corporate television and works in video production in Dallas. She holds degrees from the University of Texas at Austin and Southern Methodist University.

Ms. Ryan is single, comes from a big family of fourth-generation Texans, and currently lives in the Lakewood section of Dallas.

She wrote the Introduction to this book, along with the chapters on the prairie and the pioneers of native plant gardening in Texas.

Julie Ryan

233